BRITISH POTTERY

BRITISH POTTERY

An Illustrated Guide

Geoffrey A. Godden

Barrie & Jenkins
London

1 3.00. P

© 1974 Geoffrey A. Godden
First published 1974 by
Barrie & Jenkins Limited
24 Highbury Crescent
London N5 1RX

Designed by Michael R. Carter

Colour origination by Colour Workshop Ltd., Hertford
Filmset in Photon Times 10 on 11 pt. by
Richard Clay (The Chaucer Press), Ltd., Bungay, Suffolk
and printed in Great Britain by
The Anchor Press, Tiptree, Essex

ISBN 0 214 20034 5

Contents

The Illustrations are arranged within the following broad group-headings, in chronological order:—

Contents

Preface

This book is a companion to *British Porcelain: An Illustrated Guide*. The two works cover the whole field of British ceramics from the seventeenth century to the present-time. In these two related books the reader will find displayed nearly twelve hundred helpful and clear illustrations, mostly of objects not featured in other books.

This very large selection of illustrations has been chosen to show typical (or marked and dated) examples of the different wares or periods discussed and to show characteristic shapes or styles of decoration. These range from seventeenth-century slip-ware to 'Art Deoo' objeots of the thirties and to modern 'Studio Pottery', from documentary museum pieces to marmalade-pots, from costly specimens to inexpensive Edwardian bedroom jugs and basins. All have been selected to instruct and to give a picture of British pottery production.

As a firm believer in the value of well-chosen instructive illustrations, rather than in lengthy and often misleading written descriptions, I have placed the emphasis—as the title suggests—on the wide range of illustrations. At the same time each section has a helpful brief explanatory text and a short list of the available specialist books for the reader who wishes to delve deeply into the subject.

Acknowledgements

The display of so complete a range of instructive illustrations has only been possible through the ready co-operation of many auctioneers, dealers, present-day manufacturers, and a host of private collectors. The names of these persons are listed below in alphabetical order, next to which will be found the reference number of the illustration, or illustrations, supplied. In the case of items credited to firms of auctioneers or to dealers it will be appreciated that the articles are probably not now in their possession. Apart from acknowledging my debt, such a list does show the type of article which these firms have on offer or, in the case of dealers, items or classes of ware which they may reasonably be expected to stock. Such commercial firms have the prefix 'Messrs' together with the city or town in which the business is situated. Pottery manufacturing firms have the prefix 'Messrs' but no town is mentioned.

Messrs A. F. Allbrook, London, 53, 55.

Mrs M. Allen, 379.

M. Anderson, Esq., 381.

W. S. Arnold, Esq., 258.

Miss C. J. Ault, 447–52.

Miss M. A. Ball, 283.

M. S. Ball, Esq., 305–7.

Val Barry, 581.

Martin Battersby, Esq., 525–26.

C. Beach, Esq., 316, 318, 320, 322, 326.

S. M. Bennett, Esq., 330.

Messrs J. Bourne, 584–85.

Mrs M. S. Bourne, 221.

The British Council, 571.

H. Browne, Esq., 286–87, 289.

Miss J. M. Browne, 115.

Messrs Burgess & Leigh, 594–95.

Mr and Mrs G. Butcher, 284.

Messrs Christie, Manson & Woods Ltd., 3, 13, 15, 38, 143, 147–49, 191, 193, 227, 279, 438, 457.

Messrs Coalport China Co. Ltd., 319.

C. Collins, Esq., 525–26.

Messrs Richard Dennis, London, 409, 414, 469, 551, 553, Colour Plate XV.

Messrs Doulton & Co. Ltd., 410, 597.

Miss M. Dunne, 390–91.

Messrs A. Filkins, London, 547.

Miss G. Forester, 482.

Miss S. Francis, 357.

Messrs Franciscan Tableware, 598.

S. A. Gardner, Esq., 254.

Messrs R. Gentle, Milton-Lilbourne, Wilts, 77, 244.

Mr and Mrs W. Gilmore, 185.

J. S. Goddard, Esq., 184.

Mr and Mrs G. Godden, 1, 24, 76, 171–72, 174, 217, 296, 298, 327–29, 331–32, 334, 341–45, 348, 353, 359, 360, 362–63, 402–3, 405–6, 412, 415, 418, 421, 441, 464, 467, 495, 499, 500, 503, 562, 566–68, 572–80, 586, 588–89, 593, Colour Plates XI, XIV, XVII, XVIII.

Mrs L. Godden, 537.

Messrs Godden of Worthing Ltd., Worthing (incorporating 'Geoffrey Godden, Chinaman'), 28, 47, 51, 67, 71–75, 95, 114, 127, 135–38, 144, 151–59, 161, 164–68, 173, 181–82, 187–90, 202–3, 205–8, 210, 212, 215–16, 218–19, 222, 224–26, 233–34, 236–40, 242, 246–47, 250–53, 255, 259–60, 262–66, 269,

Acknowledgements

Messrs Godden of Worthing Ltd. (*cont.*)
  271–73, 277–78, 280–81, 288, 290,
  294, 301–2, 304, 308–13, 317, 337,
  346, 349, 364, 368–69, 371–72, 376,
  388–89, 392–93, 395, 408, 417, 468,
  480, 483, 542, 546, 548–49, 554,
  Colour Plates II, VI, VII, IX, X, XII.
Mrs A. Godfrey, 64, 66, 69.
J. Godfrey, Esq., 25.
G. S. Godwin, Esq., 335–36, 338–40.
Messrs T. G. Green, 587.
Mr and Mrs M. G. Guest, 556.
Miss A. Harding, 223.
Mr and Mrs I. T. Henderson, 22, Colour
  Plate I.
John High, Esq., 297.
Mr and Mrs David Holgate, 209.
Messrs Hostess Tableware Ltd., 592.
S. M. Houseman, Esq., 524, Colour Plate
  XVI.
S. Huggins, Esq., 394.
Miss E. Husband, 314–15, 324.
Messrs Martin Hutton, Battle, 162.
S. James, Esq., 386–87.
Messrs Mercy Jeboult, Pershore, 195.
Messrs Jellinek & Sampson, London, 41,
  45–46, 50, 52, 54, 68, 82, 84–85, 93,
  96–97, 110, 118–19, 124, 126, 133–34,
  176–77, 179–80, 382, Colour Plate V.
C. Kellam, 582.
S. H. Leal, Esq., 383–85.
W. Leather, Esq., 470.
H. Leigh, Esq., 411.
M. G. Leigh, Esq., 175.
Messrs Liberty & Co. Ltd., 455–56,
  458–60, 511, 514.
W. L. Little, Esq., 70.
Mrs F. Lomas, 398–99.
Miss K. Long, 274, 276.
Mr and Mrs S. J. MacAlpine, 397.
Mr and Mrs J. MacCarthy, 533.
S. Machin, Esq., 291.
Miss J. Magness, 550.
Messrs D. M. & P. Manheim, London, 42,
  170.
S. Manners, Esq., 373–74.
S. A. Marsh, Esq., 241.
R. A. Martin, Esq., 94.
Messrs Mason's Ironstone China Ltd., 267,
  599.

Mrs A. May, 552.
A. S. Maynard, Esq., 366–67.
Mrs Medhurst, 564.
Mrs B. Methold, 261.
Messrs Midwinter, 596.
Messrs Minton Ltd., 370, 478.
Capt. H. A. Morgan, 214.
J. S. Morgan, Esq., 211.
T. A. Morgan, Esq. 413.
M. S. Morley, Esq., 354–56, 358.
Mrs S. G. Murch, 295.
Messrs David Newbon, London, 27, 83, 99,
  123, 128, 145, 183.
Miss W. Newman, 407.
Mrs A. North, 510.
Messrs Parke-Bernet Galleries Inc., New
  York, 141, 228.
Capt. L. A. Pascall, 248–49.
A. Pellings, Esq., 375.
Messrs Poole Pottery Ltd., 600–601.
L. N. Rose, Esq., 268–70.
Rous Lench Coll, 5, 65.
P. Shand-Kydd, Esq., 602–3.
John Solly, Esq., 557.
Messrs Sotheby & Co., 32, 33, 40, 49,
  81, 86, 90, 98, 100, 102–9, 111–13,
  117, 121, 130–32, 142, 146, 150,
  163, 192, 196–97, 199, 201, 204, 229,
  232, 235, 292, 377–78, 422, 427,
  561.
Messrs Sotheby's—Belgravia, 160, 351,
  419, 423, 425–26, 428, 431, 437, 440,
  445–46, 453, 463, 465, 494, 496–97,
  501, 512–13.
Mr and Mrs S. Stone, 14.
F. L. Sutton, Esq., 439.
Messrs Taylor & Kent, 583.
Messrs Tilley & Co. Ltd., London, 39.
Mrs W. Tree, 347, 350.
Messrs F. Turner, Horsham, 333.
Messrs J. Waring, Brighton, 285.
Mrs M. L. Waterson, 454.
Messrs Henry Watson's Potteries Ltd.,
  590–91.
F. R. Webster, Esq., 275.
Messrs Josiah Wedgwood & Sons Ltd., 139,
  140, 200, 299–300, 604–7.
Mr W. E. Wiltshire, II, 169.
Mrs C. A. Wood, 420, 424, 429, 430,
  Colour Plate XIII.

In addition, some collectors have expressed a wish that their name should not be recorded; in these few cases I have added to the caption 'Private Collection'.

Many other articles are from museum collections, as listed below, and I would like to thank their Directors, Curators, and Heads of Department for their ready co-operation.

Auckland Institute & Museum, New Zealand, 34–35.

Boscobel Restorations Inc., Garrison-on-Hudson, New York, 230–31.

British Museum, London, 17, 303.

Christchurch Mansion, Ipswich, 293.

City Museum & Art Gallery, Stoke-on-Trent, 6–8, 19–21, 62–63, 79, 87, 91, 101, 116, 125, 129, 213, 282.

Colonial Williamsburg, Virginia, 12, 16, 23, 43–44, 59, 88–89, 92, 120.

Conservatoire National des Arts et Métiers, Paris, 361.

Derby Museum, 178.

Fitzwilliam Museum, Cambridge, 380.

Kestner Museum, Hanover, Germany, 481.

Liverpool City Museum, 256–57.

National Museum of Ireland, Dublin, 48.

Nelson Gallery—Atkins Museum, Kansas City, 2, 4, 9–11, 29–31, 36–37, 57, 61, 78, 80, 122.

Public Record Office, London, 352.

Shrewsbury Museum, Clive House, 485–89.

Victoria & Albert Museum, London, 18, 26, 56, 58, 60, 198, 321, 323, 365, 432, 461, 484, 508, 534, 540, 560, 569, 570.

In addition, some source material such as contemporary photographs has been reproduced from the following journals, by kind permission of the editors or publishers.

The Connoisseur, 543.

The Magazine of Art, 442.

Our Homes and Gardens, 502.

Pottery Gazette, 443–44, 462, 473–74, 476, 515–23, 527–32, 535–36, 555.

The Studio, 433–36, 466, 471, 477, 479, 490–93, 498, 538–39, 541–42, 544–46, 558–59.

I am also indebted to the several photographers who have expertly taken the photographs. Many of these are unknown to me but I am especially grateful to Mr Derek Gardiner, of Worthing, who has posed and photographically recorded so many of the articles published here. On a personal note I wish to thank Mrs Malwynne Magness for interpreting, and often improving, my long-hand copy and turning it into presentable material for my publishers to digest.

Geoffrey A. Godden,
17–19 Crescent Road,
Worthing, BNI IRT,
England.

Introduction

This pictorial review of British pottery covers a period of some three hundred years, from the general acceptance of pottery on the table—largely replacing wooden trenchers and pewter plates—forward (if that is the right word) to the age of plastic.

The description 'plastic' is a very loose one, embracing in today's parlance a host of man-made materials. Yet the pottery itself is, or was, plastic, in the sense of malleable, otherwise it could not be formed on the potter's wheel or moulded into intricate forms. Pottery too is also largely man-made, in the sense that man refines the basic clay and from this and other raw materials produces objects of beauty and use.

Where then is the difference between objects of plastic clay and of the so-called man-made plastics. It certainly isn't in the baking processes and probably not so much in the mix or mixes themselves. Surely the all-important difference lies in the making, the formation, of a pottery object, for the often rough utilitarian pots which we admire so much today, the early slip-decorated earthenwares for example, were made by hand, as individual examples, perhaps turned on the potter's-wheel, the ball of clay there coaxed into a pleasing shape, one that reflected the skill and taste of the potter. It acquired *personality* and *individuality* and these are the two qualities that are so important and make the difference between pottery and mass-produced plastic objects.

Not all pottery displays these desirable characteristics; much of the later wares also lack personality and individuality, being mass-produced from impersonal moulds in much the same way that today's plastic plates or cups are pressed-out. Yet even with these later wares it is possible to find atmosphere. For example, the average Victorian Staffordshire figure (Plates 383–88), originally mass-produced from moulds, can depict a personality of the period reminding us of an historical event or pastime, and when we recall that such pieces were coloured-up by girls and boys, often not in their teens, working from dawn to dusk for a mere pittance, we should think also of the conditions under which so much of these humble wares were produced. We could also remember the poor hawkers who endeavoured to sell their low-priced pottery, be it beer-mugs or chimney ornaments, around the country markets. The most costly, sophisticated wares, the dinner services and tea services, for example, were sold in china shops of the period, but with road conditions as they were we can wonder how the housewife ever received her pottery intact. The canal system, pioneered to a great extent by Josiah Wedgwood, was a boon to the potters, and a large percentage of the incoming raw materials and the finished pottery travelled by water, by canal and coastal shipping.

The general arrangement of this book is in chronological order, of the different types of ware as they were introduced and improved upon. There was, of course, a degree of overlap; the slip-ware potters were producing their charming wares at the same time that the London, Liverpool, and Bristol potters were producing their tin-glazed Delft-type earthenware. Also many potters produced at the same time several different classes of ware, creamware, basalt, and jasper for example.

13

With the early wares, those produced before about 1750, our pictorial representation is somewhat distorted, for the pieces that have been preserved are largely of a special character. The ornamental objects, the 'drawing-room wares' and the inscribed presentation pieces tend to be preserved, while the everyday objects, the plates, tankards, jugs, and kitchen wares are apt to be discarded over the years as they become damaged in use, when fashions change or when new improvements outmode the old wares. In fact, this natural tendency is evident even in quite late wares and it is often surprisingly difficult to find today utilitarian pottery of the 1900–1920 period, whereas the ornamental wares of the same period have been lovingly cherished!

In this brief introductory section it is convenient and appropriate to discuss in general the questions of marks, origin, and age. A mark does not make a badly designed object good, and conversely the absence of a mark does not detract from the visual beauty of an object. A mark can, however, be a great help in accurately identifying the maker of a given object and in many cases the date of production can also be ascertained by reference to one of the standard mark-books such as my *Encyclopaedia of British Pottery and Porcelain Marks* (Herbert Jenkins, London, 1964). While most collectors would rather have a marked specimen than an unmarked one, it is not a vital part of collecting and, as it happens, seven of the rather special objects which I have selected to illustrate in colour are devoid of a maker's mark. In fact, it is the exception rather than the rule to find marks on whole classes of pottery, for example salt-glaze wares, creamwares, lustre-decorated wares, Staffordshire figures, while one should even go so far as to cast doubts on any marked pottery of the types made before about 1760, the slip-decorated wares, the tin-glazed Delft-type wares, the early stonewares, and the like. A short explanation on the dating of marks is given on page 441, while other marks are given in the relevant text, for example the basic Wedgwood marks are mentioned in that section, on page 114.

The origin of a piece gives concern to many. They ask 'Is it Staffordshire?' 'Is it Leeds?', but unless for some reason one has purposefully limited oneself to the study of a single factory or class of ware, such questions are of little importance. Not everything made in the complex now known as the Staffordshire Potteries is praiseworthy, far from it. In the nineteenth century, especially, for every well-run pottery turning out good-quality, well-designed earthenware there were twenty or more small back-street 'pot-banks' employing five or six persons (or commonly children of nine or ten years of age) in dreadful conditions for long hours, for very little remuneration. These back-street 'potteries' were concerned only with producing wares down to a price, cutting out in the process all pretence to design or quality. At the time these wares found a market because of their low price, but we do not have to worship them today just because they are 'Staffordshire'. Similarly, a good piece of Bristol earthenware may be more praiseworthy than an ordinary example from the fashionable Leeds factory. In citing these examples I mean no disrespect to the Staffordshire Potteries or to the Leeds wares, I merely wish to point out that instead of asking 'Is it Staffordshire?' or 'Is it Leeds?', the collector should ask 'Is it well designed and functional?', 'Is it good quality?', or 'Do I like it for what it is?'.

Turning to age, an 'antique' is now generally accepted as an object over a hundred years old, and many people revere the almost-magic word 'antique'. But age in itself is not a virtue! A poorly designed mass-produced horror does not become a thing of beauty as soon as it reaches its hundredth birthday. The only thing that changes is our taste and our attitude to an object or its period. In this book I have disregarded age and have shown a representative selection of British pottery from the seventeenth century to the 1970s. These various wares have different attributes, they were made to suit vastly different conditions, by potters of varying talents and with different objects in mind. The manufacturers ranged from humble country potters with few or no helpers, to huge commercial concerns like the Wedgwood complex, turning out wares not only for the home market but for practically every country of the world.

From this vast cross-section we must make our own choice of what we like or dislike, of what we choose to study and collect, or with what we ornament our homes. Our home often dictates our choice: a thatched country cottage calls for oak furniture and with this the pottery of the period cannot be bettered, the slip-decorated earthenwares, or the tin-glazed Delft-style pottery, or at a lower price range the blue-printed Staffordshire earthenware, even the much despised Willow-pattern looks at home and in keeping. Strangely, the Victorian earthenware figures and dogs marry in well with oak furniture and with the cottage-style of furniture, as does the warm, friendly-looking copper-lustre coated earthenware.

Turning from country cottage to city flats, often furnished rather sparsely in the modern mode, currently produced studio pottery can be most effective. Typical specimens are shown in this special section (page 408) and the range is almost limitless. Curiously the designs of the 1920s can still be very striking, not merely the Art Deco-styled pieces (page 385 but the more orthodox wares of the period—examples are Pilkington's Royal Lancastrian wares (Plates 494–503) and the Wedgwood wares designed by Keith Murray (Plate 534).

In presenting this illustrated guide to British Pottery, with its selection of wares chosen to show characteristic specimens, not necessarily especially beautiful or costly pieces, I submit that our potters have, often unknowingly, produced a range of pottery unrivalled by any nation. Wares often humble and utilitarian that have been exported to all parts of the world and enjoyed by generation after generation, not only of collectors but, more importantly, of users. I trust that generations to come will continue to enjoy and benefit from the skill of past, present, and future British Potters.

Slip-wares

Slip-decorated earthenware is not confined to the Staffordshire Potteries, it is an early standard form of embellishing ordinary clay-colour pottery with one or more surface coatings of a more refined (or coloured) clay. The term 'slip' describes clay diluted with water to approximately the consistency of cream, although for an overall dip it could be nearer the consistency of milk.

The basic technique is shown in the factory waster (Plate I) of a dish (such as that shown in Plate 25). The dish or other object is formed of often low-quality inexpensive clay, this is then coated with a thin slip of a normally whitish refined clay to hide the inferior brick-coloured body. On this surface slip various designs can be trailed-on with different coloured slips by means of a special but simple slip-trailer. One of the simplest modes of decoration is seen on this waster—lines of brown trailed-slip are pulled by drawing a bristle or similar thin object across the lines forming a pleasing series of loops (see Plates 1, 7, 18, and 25). Dr Plot in his 1686 *Natural History of Staffordshire* wrote perhaps from first-hand knowledge

> '... they slip or paint them, with their severall sorts of slip, according as they designe their work; when the first slip is dry, laying on the others at their leisure, the orange slip making the ground, and the white and red the paint; which two colours they break with a wire brush, much after the manner they doe when they marble paper....'

This is, however, far from the full story. Many designs, including the famous Toft-type wares are simply and charmingly drawn with trailed-slip, often in a naïve manner (Plates 2–6). These dishes are intriguing, they can hardly have been made for daily use, and if they were purely ornamental they represent the first British purely decorative pottery. A problem arises from the conspicuous placing of the potter's name on the front, and some persons question if these names represent the potter at all. Nevertheless, they are now rare and costly objects and are seldom found in a perfect state. While Thomas Toft is the most famous name associated with these slip-trailed wares (normally circular dishes as Plates 2–4), several other names occur: James Toft, Ralph Toft, and other surnames, William Talor, for example (Plate 5), and Ralph Simpson (Plates 9–10).

At, or near, Wrotham in Kent an interesting class of dark-bodied earthenware was decorated with light-coloured slip-decoration including inscriptions and dates. Here the potters 'signed' their work with their initials: examples by Thomas Ifield and George Richardson are shown in Plates 13–16. A helpful paper on the Wrotham wares is contained in the *Transactions of the English Ceramic Circle*, vol. 3, part 2, 1954, a paper by A. J. B. Kiddell.

In contrast, some rare wares are not made by trailing slip but rather by cutting or carving through the surface layer of slip to expose the darker body below. A Wrotham example of

17

1699 is shown in Plate 17, but this technique is mainly associated with the West Country potteries. A splendid documentary example is shown in Colour Plate I and in Plate 22, depicting in carved relief a village scene in 1788. Examples of this class were made over a lengthy period, well into the nineteenth century, and at several different potteries.

The baking-dish shown in Plate 25 illustrates a traditional and simple form of slip-decorated, utilitarian ware. These dishes range in date from the early eighteenth century onwards, and modern studio-potters still find a steady market for dishes in the same vein. Such wares were made at most pottery centres.

We can conveniently include under this slip-ware heading those red (brick-like) clay wares completely covered with a blackish glossy slip (Plates 26–27). Such glossy black-ware is traditionally called 'Jackfield' after that Shropshire pottery centre, but much of this class was in fact made in Staffordshire, as excavated wasters prove.

Of all the classes of pottery to be featured subsequently in this book, the slip-decorated wares are probably the most English and the most charming. We must remember that the early examples represent the first decorative essays in our ceramic history and that the pots and dishes graced tables when most persons ate from wooden trenchers or from pewter dishes and plates.

National and provincial museums include a good selection of early slip-wares, in particular the British Museum and the Victoria & Albert Museum in London. Of the provincial museums I will name the City Museum & Art Gallery, Stoke-on-Trent, and the Brighton Museum, but the choice is wide.

Most general reference-books contain basic information on these wares, but R. G. Cooper's *English Slipware Dishes, 1650–1850* (Tiranti, London, 1968) is an interesting specialist book (the same author's paper on Toft-type wares is contained in the *Transactions of the English Ceramic Circle*, vol. 6, part 1, 1965), and Arnold Mountford, the Director of the Stoke Museum & Art Gallery, is preparing a promising work on the subject.

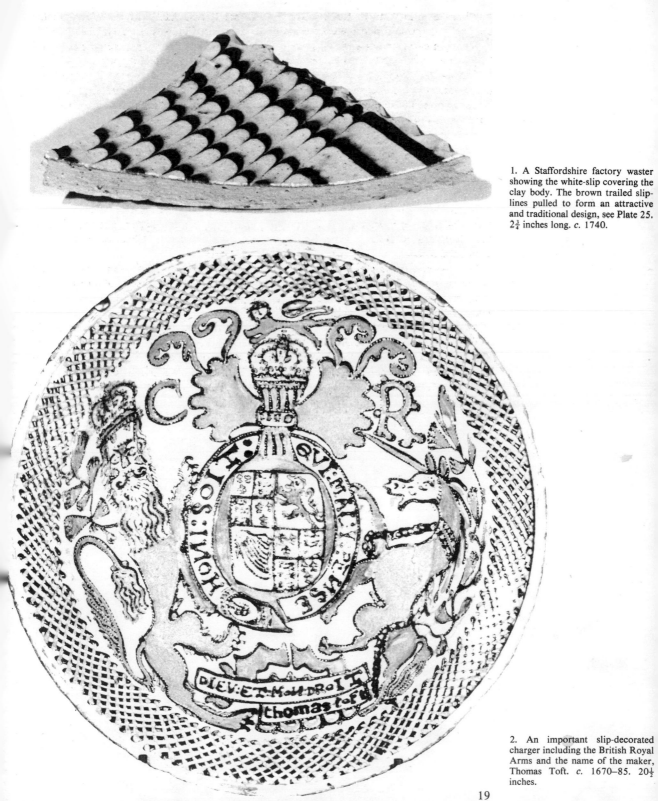

1. A Staffordshire factory waster showing the white-slip covering the clay body. The brown trailed slip-lines pulled to form an attractive and traditional design, see Plate 25. 2¾ inches long. *c.* 1740.

2. An important slip-decorated charger including the British Royal Arms and the name of the maker, Thomas Toft. *c.* 1670–85. 20½ inches.

3. An attractive Staffordshire slip-decorated charger by Thomas Toft. Note the typical trellis-like border. *c.* 1680–90. 17¾ inches.

4. An important Staffordshire slip-decorated charger, inscribed 'Thomas Toft' and bearing a representation of William III. *c.* 1690. 18¾ inches.

5. An interesting Staffordshire slip-decorated dish 'signed' by William Talor, one of the several potters who worked in this traditional style. *c.* 1675–85.

6. A rare slip-decorated earthenware charger 'signed' and dated 'Ralpph (sic) Toft. 1677'. Ralph was born *c.* 1638 and his wares are even rarer than those bearing Thomas Toft's name. 14⅝ inches diameter.

7. A Staffordshire slip-ware cup with combed decoration as Plate 1. Dated 1695. Several similar examples are recorded. 4½ inches high.

8. An amusing but simple Staffordshire slip-decorated dish. This example, like much slip-ware, is damaged, and few perfect pieces will now be encountered. Diameter 13¾ inches. *c.* 1740.

9. A rare Staffordshire slip-ware dish bearing the name Ralph Simson (a 'p' is included in the dish shown below). Diameter $17\frac{3}{4}$ inches. *c.* 1680–90.

10. A fine, large Staffordshire slip-decorated dish by Ralph Simpson. The female figure is believed to represent Queen Catherine. Diameter 18 inches. *c.* 1690.

11. A press-moulded dish, the outline coloured-in with coloured slip. The initials S.M. relate to Samuel Malkin, who specialised in this mode of manufacture. Diameter 16½ inches. *c.* 1720.

12. A rare Staffordshire slip-ware dish bearing the name and date 'John Wright, 1704'. Diameter 18¼ inches.

previous page
Colour Plate I. The side-view of the 1778 slip-decorated jug shown in Plate 22. This view depicts the church at Sandford. Inscribed 'William Holmade. Sandford. July 17th 1778'. Other jugs of this type and with similar handles bear Barnstaple or Bideford place names. 10¼ inches high.
M. T. Henderson collection.

Colour Plate III. Side-view of the salt-glazed stoneware tankard shown in Plate 66. The unusual feature of this popular Hogarth's 'Midnight Modern Conversation' tankard is the manner in which the horse and dogs are picked out in manganese. Inscribed 'Jno Thompson' and dated 1729. 8⅛ inches high.

Colour Plate II. A decorative and popular polychrome delft design found on plates and circular dishes. Lambeth, mid-18th century. Diameter 12 inches.

following page
Colour Plate IV. A superb Staffordshire salt-glazed coffee, or chocolate, pot, with the spout at right angles to the handle. The style of painting and palette is typical of its type and period in the late 1750s or early 1760s. 8¼ inches high.

Private Collection

A conventional coffee pot decorated by the same hand is shown as Plate 180 in Arnold Mountford's *The Illustrated Guide to Staffordshire Salt-Glazed Stoneware* (1971).

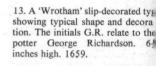

13. A 'Wrotham' slip-decorated tyg showing typical shape and decoration. The initials G.R. relate to the potter George Richardson. 6½ inches high. 1659.

14. A further Wrotham tyg bearing the date 1649 and the initials T.I. These initials are attributed to the potter Thomas Ifield and other initialled examples range between 1631 and 1654. 6½ inches high.

15. A fine and rare Wrotham slip-decorated flagon by George Richardson (see Plate 13). Dated 1651. $9\frac{3}{4}$ inches high.

16. A pair, perhaps unique, of Wrotham slip-decorated candlesticks, each dated 1668 and attributed to George Richardson (see Plates 13 and 15). $10\frac{7}{8}$ inches high.

17. A Wrotham earthenware dish dated 1699 with the makers initials I.E. for John Eaglestone. The covering slip has been cut or carved away in a technique normally associated with the West Country, rather than with the Kent wares. Diameter $21\frac{1}{2}$ inches.

18. An attractive but simple Staffordshire slip-trailed and 'combed' jug, dated 1701. 4¼ inches high.

19. A Staffordshire slip-decorated cradle—a popular object—by Ralph Shaw. 11½ inches long. *c.* 1730.

20. A rare Staffordshire slip-decorated egg-stand, with tulip motifs. *c.* 1700. 3⅝ inches high.

21. A rather late Staffordshire slip-decorated dish, dated 1749 and made at a time when the lighter and almost white salt-glazed stonewares were in fashion. Diameter 13½ inches.

22. The Front-view of a unique documentary jug, the covering slip cut away to form a view of the West Country village of Sandford with the Rose & Crown as it appeared in 1778. Incise'd Inscription 'made by Joseph Rice'. See also colour plate I. $10\frac{3}{4}$ inches high.

23. A carved, scratched or 'sgraffito'-decorated beer-jug of West Country origin, inscribed 'by Jos. Hollamore' and dated 27 June 1764. $14\frac{1}{2}$ inches high.

24. A small slip-decorated dish of recent date showing that this technique is not confined to antique specimens. $4\frac{1}{2}$ inches. 1968.

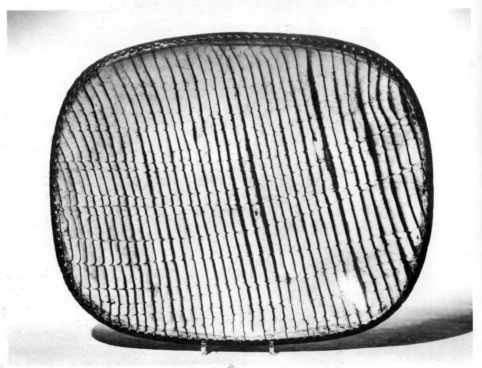

25. A shallow slip-decorated, combed baking dish of a traditional type made over two hundred and fifty years ago. 18 × 14 inches.

26. A simple but forceful Jackfield-type slip-covered earthenware jug, dated 1776. Probably Staffordshire. 8 inches high.

27. A group of so-called Jackfield black-glazed earthenware pots, almost certainly of Staffordshire origin. *c.* 1750–60. Coffee pot 9¼ inches high.

Delft-type Wares

These so-called delft-type wares are related to the English slip-wares in one important aspect; both techniques are basically a mode of covering an inferior clay-coloured body with a thin film of a superior nature, to hide and enhance the underlying ware. With the English delftwares (a small 'd' is used where we refer to the imitations of the famous Dutch Delft prototypes) the covering layer is a form of white glaze containing tin-ashes as a whitening agent, hence the term 'tin-glaze'. While it is general practice to name our tin-glazed earthenwares delftware, the early examples are more related in general style to the other Continental tin-glazed maiolica-type wares or 'faience', and there is a school of thought that believes the term 'English-maiolica' should be used.

Tin-glazed earthenware has, in use, two basic faults. The underlying clay body is rather friable and the covering glaze is very prone to chipping or to cracking, so that in daily use it soon became unsightly and unhygienic—owing to the exposed body absorbing liquids. It was, however, until the early 1700s the nearest our potters could get to emulating white porcelain, and many examples were made in the style of the fashionable Chinese and Japanese porcelains. Plate 28 shows typical edge-chipping and glaze-flaking to be found on old delftwares. Nevertheless, from the collector's point of view they are charming, decorative, historically interesting, and rare.

There were in this country several centres of the tin-glaze pottery industry—London, Bristol, Liverpool, Glasgow, and Wincanton, but surprisingly it does not appear to have been made in the Staffordshire potteries, although the introduction in Staffordshire of their superior cream-coloured ware (page 140) was to cause the closure of the delft potteries.

One of the most interesting products of the London potteries was the series of pill-slabs and apothecaries' drug-jars (Plate 29). In fact, this trade—with the multitude of little pots—must have been the mainstay of the London potters in the seventeenth and early eighteenth centuries. Another staple object was the wine or sack bottle. These charming objects were normally plain, as those seen in Plate 33, but very occasionally special inscribed and even armorial examples were made (Plate 31). The reader is warned that reproductions have been made. Purely decorative pieces such as the 1657 pictorial charger seen in Plate 32 and the seemingly popular, relief-moulded 'La Fécondité' dishes (Plate 35) were the exception; most tin-glazed English delftware is of a useful nature and much has perished over the years.

An historically interesting class of 'blue-dash' charger (named after the characteristic blue-dash border-design), however, had a relatively high survival rate, perhaps because such pieces were regarded as more decorative than functional. Several of these chargers depict Royalty, drawn in the pleasing, spontaneous manner necessitated by painting on the extremely porous tin-glaze before it was fired. A good range of these 'portrait' chargers is shown in Plates 36–38. Several other decorative motifs were employed such as 'Adam & Eve' (Plates 41–42) and simple floral designs. (See a paper by R. H. Warren in the *Transactions of the English Ceramic Circle*, vol. 1, no. 4, 1937.)

34

The ornate posset-pots in Plate 44 are among the most unusual objects to be found, though many have now lost their covers, handles, and spouts. Other characteristic delft-ware articles are the so-called 'bricks' or flower-containers, a good selection of which are shown in Plate 52. Tiles, of course, formed a staple line for the delftware potters although the Dutch ones were imported in great quantities.

While I have previously listed the main British centres of this pottery, some wares were also made in Ireland, mainly in Dublin. Sample illustrations of such wares are shown in Plates 47–49.

By the 1760s the production of tin-glazed pottery in England had suffered a decline owing to the superior qualities of white salt-glazed stonewares and of the new cream-coloured ware, and by the 1780s it had practically ceased. Even the Continental potters were nearly all forced to turn to the manufacture of the new English-style creamware—so much superior in use.

The correct attribution of tin-glazed delft-type pottery is difficult and quite impossible to explain in this brief summary. Specialist books such as F. H. Garner's *English Delftware* (Faber & Faber, London, 1948, enlarged and revised by Michael Archer, 1972) or Anthony Ray's *English Delftware Pottery* (Faber & Faber, London, 1968) offer the reader helpful guidance, together with a good range of illustrations. Painting a broad picture, there is also Alan Caiger-Smith's *Tin-glaze Pottery in Europe and the Islamic World* (Faber & Faber, London, 1973). Such books, however, cannot compete with the constant handling of documentary specimens—a near impossible ideal!—but a good range of examples are at least on view, at the Victoria & Albert Museum, London, and at the Ashmolean Museum, Oxford, for example.

28. Detail of a tin-glazed delft-type pot showing the typical edge chipping and the underlying clay-coloured body.

29. A Lambeth delftware pill-slab bearing the arms of the Apothecaries' Company and the City of London with a similar drug-jar. Many apothecary jars were made in various styles in these tin-glazed wares but some are of Continental origin. Jar 11 inches high. *c.* 1680–1700.

30. A rare silver-mounted London delftware jug of the type known as 'Malling jugs' and a rare Southwark type mug decorated in blue and dated 1629. 4⅞ inches high. *c.* 1600, and 1629.

31. A fine London (Lambeth) delftware 'Sack' bottle decorated in blue. Inscribed 'Wm Allen' and dated 1647. Most delftware bottles of this type are very simply decorated, see Plate 33. 6⅛ inches high.

32. A unique London (Southwark) delft charger. The initials (in the sky—centre) are believed to relate to Richard and Elizabeth Newnham, Master potters of St Olave's, Southwark. This charger has been repaired since this photograph was taken and is to be seen in the Victoria & Albert Museum, London. Diameter 18¼ inches. Dated 1657.

33. A selection of three rare dated, but typical, London delftware handled 'bottles' or flagons. 6¼ to 7½ inches high.

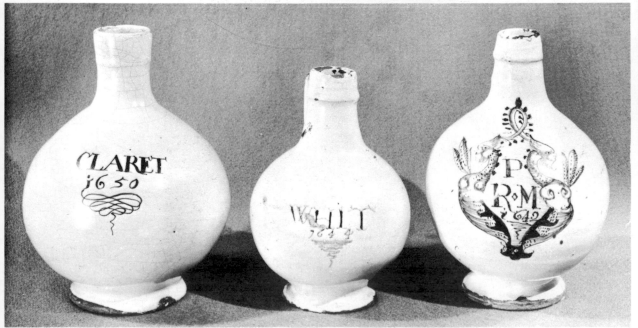

34. Detail of inscription incorporated in the elaborate delftware dish shown below, The inscription reads 'Isaac Hickson, Anno Dom 1658', but other similar dishes bear dates between 1633 and 1697.

35. A relief-moulded London (Lambeth) delftware dish showing a popular design, but decorated in an unusually ornate manner after a French Bernard Palissy original after Titian's 'La Fécondité'. Dated 1658. 19 inches long.

39

36. A rare Lambeth delftware 'blue-dash' charger, perhaps commemorating the coronation of Charles II in 1661. Diameter 12½ inches.

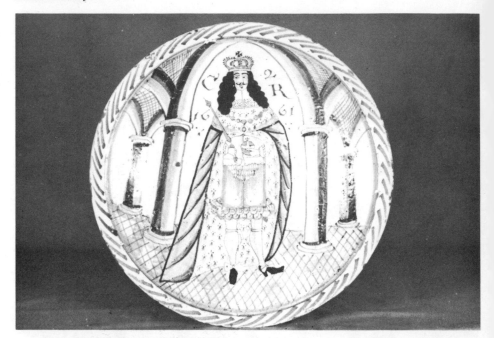

37. A powerfully painted 'blue-dash' charger dated 1672. Probably Lambeth and depicting Catherine of Braganza. Diameter 13 inches.

Opposite page

38. A rare selection of blue-dash and related tin-glazed delft chargers depicting from top-left to bottom-right—William and Mary, William III, The Duke of Marlborough, Prince George, and Prince Eugene. *c.* 1690–1720. Prince Eugene charger 13¾ inches diameter.

39. A good Lambeth tin-glazed posset-pot of typical form, painted in blue and inscribed 'Daniel Cock, 1682'. $7\frac{1}{2}$ inches high.

40. A rare, early Bristol delft plate bearing the owner's initials and date 1679. Diameter $7\frac{3}{4}$ inches.

41. A typical Bristol delft blue-dash Adam and Eve charger. *c.* 1700.

42. A rare initialled and dated, 1741, Bristol delft Adam and Eve large polychrome charger. Diameter 12¾ inches.

Following pages

43. A rare Lambeth delft two-handled, urn-shaped vase decorated in blue with Chinese-style motifs. 8 inches high. *c.* 1700.

44. An ornate tin-glazed posset-pot decorated with polychrome colours. Probably of Bristol origin. 13¼ inches high. Early 18th century.

45. A charming Lambeth delft blue and white plate in the popular Chinese taste. Diameter 8½ inches. *c.* 1740.

Opposite page

47. A rare Dublin delft low basket painted in blue in a characteristic manner. J. K. monogram-mark. Diameter 9 inches. *c.* 1755.

48. A rare Irish tin-glazed delft-type shoe-ornament, dated 1724. The Irish potters favoured these shoes but some are of English make. Length 5½ inches.

46. A rare, but typical Bristol delft bowl. The interior painted with a road-mending scene. *c.* 1750.

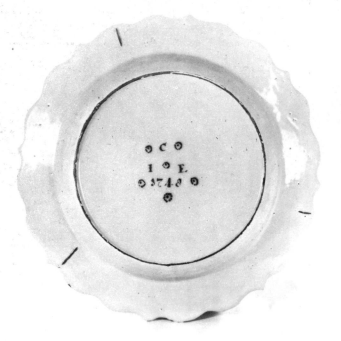

49. The reverse and front of a rare Irish delft plate dated 1748 and attributed to Crisp's Dublin factory. Diameter 8⅞ inches.

50. A Liverpool delft plate bearing the initials of the owner and the date 1753. Diameter 8½ inches.

51. A pair of blue-painted tin-glazed plates painted with a typical Chinese-style floral design. Both are inscribed and dated on the reverse side. Diameter 8¾ inches.

52. A selection of tin-glazed 'bricks', a popular flower-holder seemingly made only by the British delftware potters, noticeably at Bristol and Liverpool. Average length 6 inches. *c.* 1750–60.

53. A rare relief-moulded Liverpool delftware cornucopia-shaped wall-pocket decorated in polychrome. *c.* 1755–60.

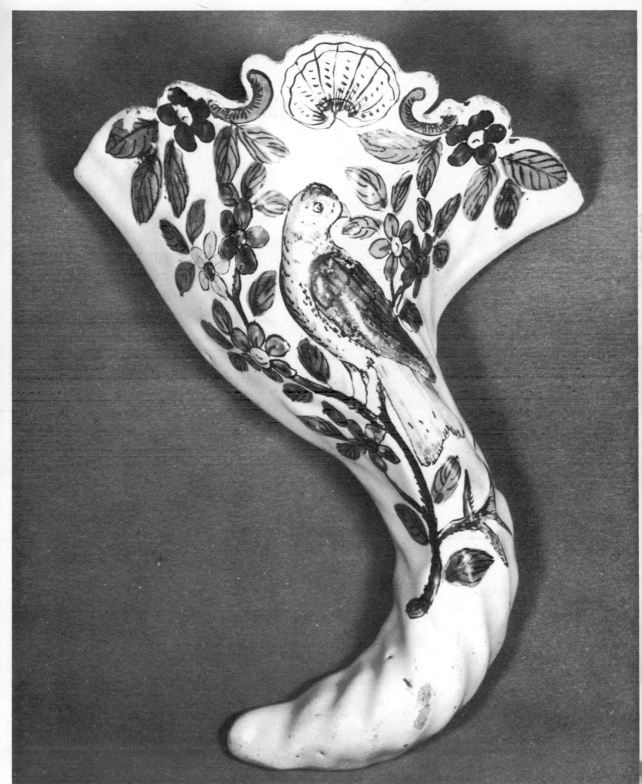

54. A decorative Bristol delft plate, the white border-design being known as 'Bianco sopra Bianco', *c.* 1750. Diameter 8¼ inches.

55. A large Bristol delft dish, simply decorated in polychrome. *c.* 1750–55. Diameter 10¾ inches.

Stonewares

In the two previous sections we have discussed relatively low-fired friable and porous earthenwares which, for table use, needed to be covered with a sealing glaze. We now turn to high-fired vitrified durable stoneware, fired to the 1200° to 1400° centigrade range so that it is impervious to liquids.

The manufacture of English stoneware is not confined to any one district, but its development and perfection can be said to have taken place in London in the early 1670s. The Fulham potter concerned was John Dwight (*c.* 1639–1703) and his first patent for the manufacture of 'transparent earthenware commonly called porcellane or china' was taken out in April 1672 after earlier experiments near Wigan. His boast was no idle one, for within a short period his finished wares had attracted attention and Robert Hooke was able to note in his diary—'Saw Mr. Dwight's English China, Dr. Willis his head, a little boye with a hawke on his fist, severall little jarrs of severall colours all exceeding hard as a flint. Very light, of very good shape. The performance very admirable and out doing any European potters' (entry of 17 February 1674). Recently discovered wasters on the Fulham Pottery site include parts of German-style stoneware bottles with decorative embossed panels, including the early date 1674.

Dwight's products are indeed remarkable for their period—the figures (Plate 56) are without parallel, and the variegated mugs and jugs (probably Hooke's 'little jarrs of severall colours') are neat, robust, and attractive (see Plates 57–58). Hooke's description 'hard as a flint' is also noteworthy, for he later recorded that Dwight used powdered flint in his mix, and in this he must have been the first to incorporate in the body this later standard ingredient.

Francis Place was a little-known contemporary of Dwight. A good account of his life and work is given in a paper by R. E. G. Tyler, published in the *Transactions of the English Ceramic Circle*, vol. 8, part 2, 1972.

The uneven orange-skin-like glaze seen especially in Plate 58 is due to the salt used as a glazing agent when introduced to the kiln during firing, and most subsequent stoneware is salt-glazed. John Dwight's unmarked stoneware was ahead of its time and reputedly expensive—examples are now mainly preserved in national museums, but his work is not as respected as it should be. He lifted English pottery from a peasant craft to a higher plane, one approaching Oriental porcelain in durability, and in the quality of his figure work he led the world.

Turning from London to Nottingham we find a flourishing stoneware industry, led by James Morley, whose work can sometimes be attributed by reference to his engraved trade-card. Plates 60–61 show typical Nottingham-type stonewares.

Much stoneware was also made in the Staffordshire Potteries. A typical tankard of a type made at most stoneware centres is shown in Plate 63, fired to the side of its protective 'saggar'. This factory waster was excavated in Burslem (as was the tankard shown in

Plate 62). The large holes cut in the side of the 'saggar' were to enable the volatile salt-fumes to reach and glaze the ware during the firing. Tankards of this type often had official capacity-seals impressed into the body—these can help to date an otherwise almost timeless article—for example the tankard shown in Plate 62 bears a Queen Anne seal, while that shown in Plate 64 bears a Georgian 'G.R.' seal.

Noble stoneware 'Hogarth' tankards such as that shown in Colour Plate III and in Plate 66, were apparently popular gifts, for surprising numbers with incised names and dates have survived—in varying states! The one shown here is a superb example of its class. The relief-decoration was made in separate moulds and 'sprigged' on (in the manner of the later Wedgwood reliefs), but for their early eighteenth-century date they are splendidly typical products of the English potter's craft. They are normally attributed to Fulham in London, sometimes to Dwight's former pottery.

The basic form of sprigged hunting-scene—with or without the main Hogarth subject-panel, was popular at several centres over a lengthy period (Plate 74). The Nottingham potters seem to have produced similar jugs at a later date (Plate 67) and the Doulton potteries were making similar wares until recent times. The darker, dipped top-section is traditional, and occurs on nearly all examples of these 'sprigged' jugs and mugs at all periods. The jug shown in Plate 69 is a rare departure from the standard hunting-subject motif.

Some stoneware, notably the Nottingham wares, were decorated with simple incised motifs, see Plate 68. Later Nottingham 'sprigged' stonewares are shown in Plates 71–72.

While most stoneware is of a utilitarian nature, some useful vessels were given a decorative treatment. An extensive and interesting range of flasks were moulded in varied forms. That shown in Plate 75 is a pleasing example, while the front of that shown in Plate 76 depicts the young Queen Victoria. This example is unusual in that it has an impressed, dated inscription as well as the maker's mark. The stoneware potters from Bristol, also other West Country potteries, in London and up to and including Scotland made thousands of plain pots of different sizes to serve as food and other containers (ink, etc.). The superb Cooper's Orange Marmalade pot illustrated in Plate 77 serves well to commemorate this staple trade of the stoneware potters. Stoneware is still made, particularly by the present-day Studio Potters (page 408). Although most stoneware was glazed with salt, some was lead-glazed, or borax could be added to the salt, so reducing the firing temperature. This additive also resulted in a more glossy glaze, lacking the characteristic orange-skin texture of the normal salt-glazed pieces.

The stoneware collector is at present ill-served by reference-books; several give useful information, but the best coverage is still to be found in J. F. Blacker's *The A.B.C. of English Salt-glaze Stoneware from Dwight to Doulton* (Stanley Paul & Co., London, 1922).

56. Two extremely rare Dwight stoneware figures made at Fulham (London) in the third quarter of the 17th century. Other examples of this rare class are to be seen in the Victoria & Albert, and British Museums. $6\frac{1}{4}$ inches high.

57. A fine and rare salt-glazed stone-ware-covered tankard attributed to John Dwight, with applied sprig decoration. *c.* 1690. 10½ inches high.

58. A simple and rare salt-glazed stoneware-handled bottle or jar, almost certainly from John Dwight's Fulham pottery. The typical salt-glaze orange-skin-like surface is clearly seen. *c.* 1690. 6¾ inches high.

59. A simple, but robust salt-glazed stoneware silver-mounted tankard (of a shape also found in Chinese 'blanc de Chine porcelain) attributed to John Dwight's Fulham pottery, *c.* 1690. 3$\frac{1}{16}$ inches high.

60. A Nottingham stoneware tankard of a traditional type linking with James Morley's advertisement (see *An Illustrated Encyclopaedia of British Pottery and Porcelain*, Plate 447). Incised inscription 'Nottm 1703'. 3$\frac{7}{8}$ inches high.

61. A James Morley-type pierced stoneware mug and an incised, decorated mug dated 1721. Probably of Nottingham origin. $4\frac{3}{8}$ and $5\frac{1}{2}$ inches high.

62. A Staffordshire salt-glazed stoneware tankard with 'A R' capacity-seal of Queen Anne's reign. Excavated at the George Inn, Burslem. *c.* 1710. $6\frac{1}{2}$ inches high.

63. A damaged saggar containing a
typical salt-glazed stoneware tankard of the type often attributed to
Fulham (London) or Nottingham,
but excavated at Burslem in the
Staffordshire Potteries. *c.* 1710.
Saggar 8½ inches high.

64. A simple stoneware tankard with Georgian 'GR' capacity-seal. Impressed inscription 'I Brown, 1770'. $5\frac{3}{8}$ inches high.

65. A rare lipped mug, or jug, with incised inscription 'John Griffin, Dish turner in Bury St. Edmunds. January y first 1756'.

66. A fine stoneware relief-moulded large tankard (for side-view see Colour Plate III). The central panel depicting Hogarth's famous 'Midnight Modern Conversation', a very popular subject found on many tankards of this type, and used over a lengthy period. Inscribed 'Jno Thompson' and dated 1729. 8¼ inches high.

Opposite page

67. A later version of the popular Midnight Conversation hunting-jug made at various stoneware centres over a lengthy period. Compare with Plate 66. *c.* 1800. 6 inches high.

68. Two views of a typical Nottingham-type stoneware two-handled 'loving-cup', dated 1720. Such simple pieces have great charm. 7 inches high.

69. A rare and attractive stoneware jug with applied relief-motifs of an unusual type. Inscribed on the front—'William Broad, June 4th, 1792' and under the base 'W Sheppard'. 10 inches high.

70. A documentary Chesterfield stoneware jug, the side inscribed 'John Bralsford, March 29th, 1775' and under the base 'John Wright, maker, Chesterfield'. 8¼ inches high.

71. A rather late Nottingham stoneware mug, with relief motifs and
inscribed 'J Colton, New Wiseton,
Nottinghamshire. 1830'. 4 inches
high.

72. A rare Nottingham-type stoneware jug inscribed 'Joseph Bates,
1829'. 6½ inches high.

73. A West Country stoneware inkpot and pen-holder, bearing the rare mark 'Great Western Pottery. Crudleigh. Devon'. *c.* 1880. 1¾ inches high.

74. A rare Mortlake (London) relief-patterned mug, here displayed upside-down to show the impressed mark 'Kishere Pottery, Mortlake, Surrey'. Dated 1839. 4¼ inches high.

75. An attractive London stoneware flask in the form of a gun-
powder flask. Impressed mark
'Stephen Green. Imperial Potteries,
Lambeth'. Green and other potters
made many decorative moulded
bottles and flasks in novel forms. *c.*
1840–50. 9½ inches high.

A PRESANT
FROM W. FORD
TO R. F. BULL.
ASHBOURN.
AUG 19
1836.

DENBY & CODNOR PARK
BOURNES
POTTERIES
DERBYSHIRE

76. A documentary, marked Bourne's Denby & Codnor Park Derbyshire stoneware bottle in the form of the uncrowned Queen Victoria and dated 19 August 1836. See revised edition of Jewitt's *Ceramic Art of Great Britain 1800–1900* (Barrie & Jenkins, London, 1972) Plate 91, for front. 8 inches high.

77. The reverse and front view of an early Victorian Cooper's marmalade jar. Marked 'Green. Lambeth. Improved Stone ware glazed inside'. Stephen Green sold his pottery in 1858. A utilitarian object, but of great interest, for such marked pieces are now quite rare. 7¼ inches high.

Salt-glazed Wares

The stonewares featured in the previous section were in the main salt-glazed by the introduction of salt into the kilns during the firing process. However, the previously discussed stonewares were of a dark clay-colour while the wares we generally call salt-glaze, or at least Staffordshire salt-glaze, are of a refined, whitish body and delicately formed. In these two regards the potters were seeking to emulate the fashionable porcelains. It is these white, or near-white, wares which are the subject of this section.

In essence the story is concerned with the Staffordshire Potteries, although this is not to say that similar, now difficult to identify, wares were not made at other ceramic centres such as Liverpool. All white salt-glaze is difficult to attribute, certainly to any one potter, for no factory-marks occur. In one sense this is advantageous, for instead of a collector seeking the wares of one particular factory, he chooses those objects which please him, irrespective of their origins.

The standard white Staffordshire salt-glazed stoneware was probably introduced between 1710 and 1720 (a year recorded on an inscribed example). The earliest pieces were merely surface-coated with an 'englobe', a 'slip' of the expensive white clay brought from Devon and Dorset. The slightly later, standard, white Staffordshire salt-glazed body contained flint, but the introduction of flint into ceramic bodies was by no means a Staffordshire innovation (the oft-repeated story that John Astbury got the idea from an ostler curing his horse's troubled eyes is unlikely). Calcined flints had long been used in the manufacture of glass. Dwight was apparently using them for his wares in 1674 when Robert Hooke noted 'Dwight's secret consists only in flint powdered and a salt mix't with pipe-clay . . .'. Before 1700 English flints were an item of export. However, in the light of present knowledge it seems unlikely that the Staffordshire white flint-ware was introduced before 1710. The term 'flint-ware' is a useful one, being more apt than the all-embracing term 'salt-glaze', which can include brown stonewares of all types. The maker of such white wares was sometimes called a 'flint-potter'.

While the figures shown in Plates 78–80 are not the earliest examples of Staffordshire salt-glaze, they show the charming, homely nature of the ware. Although later, by some sixty years, than the Dwight figures (Plate 56) they are naïve in comparison, but they are the individual hand-made product of honest potters, not sculptors. These 'pew groups' (Plate 78) and early figures are very rare and costly, factors that have led to the manufacture of reproductions—some of which are now almost antique!

The table wares are more procurable than the figures, although both are still rare. A fine, interesting range of moulded teapots was made (Plates 83, 84, and 86) displaying little or no influence from other ceramics. They are, as a class, unique to eighteenth-century Staffordshire salt-glazed stoneware. These pots and allied wares (Plates 82, 85, 87, 88, 89, 95, 105) were cast in Plaster of Paris moulds and were at the time made in quantity. Other pieces were press-moulded, that is formed by pressing bats of clay into prepared moulds.

71

These moulds could be of metal, of fired clay, or of plaster. In general the pressed-moulded pieces are not as thin as the cast ones, nor do they show the design in reverse, inside. The cast wares were extremely thin-walled, the slip being permitted to remain in the absorbent moulds for a short time, and it is a wonder how these thin, fragile wares ever reached the buying public over the rough roads of the period. In this respect water transport was a blessing and, of course, enabled the Staffordshire potters to export their novel white Flint wares overseas.

Apart from the moulded white wares, very decorative effects were achieved by 'sprig-ging-on' relief motifs of a contrasting colour clay, Plates 90–92 show examples in this uncommon technique.

Moving forward from the white unpainted wares we come to a simple form of decoration known as 'scratch-blue' or 'scratched-blue', achieved by incising designs into the still-soft clay and then filling the indentations with pigment—normally blue. Plate 100 shows a handsome ale jug in this style, and the 1754 loving-cup (Plate 101) illustrates the typical form of a basic floral design.

Other salt-glazed stoneware was decorated in enamel colours after the initial firing. It is believed that this decoration was mainly carried out by specialist enamellers, including painters from Holland. The Warburtons of Hot Lane, Cobridge, are associated with the enamelling trade, but many others must have been likewise engaged. Much of the early enamelled salt-glazed stoneware is decorated in the fashionable Chinese style (Plates 96–99, 104), while rare pieces display European landscape- and figure-designs. The superb chocolate or coffee pot shown in Colour Plate IV illustrates well the attractive free manner of painting found on this ware—a style well suited to pottery, but perhaps out of keeping on the more sophisticated porcelain.

Printed designs, such as those seen in Plates 102–3, rarely occur on salt-glazed wares—normally plates. These prints seem to have been added outside Staffordshire, perhaps at Liverpool (although none bears the signature of the famous Sadler, see page 228) or in London.

In general white, salt-glazed, articles are small and of a useful nature, but the scope of shapes is amazing: charming, crisply moulded dishes were made in various shapes, fine sauceboats (Plate 85), jugs, and especially teapots. Cups and saucers are rarely found, probably on account of the damage they sustained, or perhaps the tens of thousands of Chinese teabowls that were imported undersold the Staffordshire products.

The white Staffordshire salt-glazed flint-ware enjoyed some sixty years of popularity—from about 1720 to about 1780, by which time the previously introduced cream-coloured earthenware, with its smooth lead-glaze, had superseded the salt-glazed flint-ware with its characteristic, hard and uneven glaze. The changeover was, however, gradual, some potters progressing to the new body well before 1780 while others had a foot in both camps and produced both salt-glaze wares and lead-glazed creamwares, sometimes using the same moulds for both bodies.

The English salt-glazed wares have great charm; they are typically English, catering for the needs of the vast middle-class population. The poorer families had to be content with coarser clay-coloured earthenwares (if they aspired to ceramic objects at all) while the richer bought porcelains—mostly Oriental imports until the English porcelain factories were able to compete from the mid-1740s onwards.

Most museums have some salt-glazed wares on display—if only a standard moulded plate (as Plate 105), but fine selections are included in the Victoria & Albert Museum in London and, of course, at the City Museum & Art Gallery at Stoke-on-Trent. Some American museums have particularly fine collections, including that at Colonial Williamsburg.

Our present knowledge of the subject is well presented in Arnold Mountford's *The Illustrated Guide to Staffordshire Salt-glazed Stoneware* (Barrie & Jenkins, London, 1971), a book which illustrates many documentary specimens and excavated factory wasters from Staffordshire sites.

78. Two very rare Staffordshire salt-glaze 'pew-groups' and a related single figure, showing the simple charm of these early figures and groups. *c.* 1740. Figure 6⅛ inches high.

79. A fine and rare Staffordshire salt-glazed, press-moulded figure of a mounted Hussar, with hand-modelled accoutrements. *c.* 1740. 8¾ inches high.

Opposite page

80. A Selection of simple, moulded, salt-glazed Staffordshire figures of the 1730–45 period. The centre example's skirt made up of fragments of wedged clays of different colours. 3¼ to 3⅞ inches high.

81. Two rare, but typical Staffordshire moulded salt-glazed cats, with hollow bodies. *c.* 1740–50. 6¼ and 6¾ inches high.

82. A charming early Staffordshire salt-glazed tea-caddy formed in a two-piece mould and inscribed 'CIA or TE herb', the spelling of tea being very unsettled in the 18th century. *c.* 1725–35. 3½ inches high.

83. A typical small-size Staffordshire salt-glazed teapot, with traces of the original 'cold' (unfired) gilding. *c.* 1740. 4 inches high.

84. An unusual moulded Staffordshire salt-glazed teapot with some colouring rubbed into the recessed design. *c.* 1740–45. 5 inches high.

Below
85. A rare and ornate, but somewhat crudely modelled, Staffordshire salt-glazed moulded sauce-boat. *c.* 1740–45. 6½ inches long.

Opposite page
86. Two rare but typical Staffordshire moulded, salt-glazed teapots, the left-hand example depicting Admiral Vernon and the taking of Portobello in 1739. *c.* 1740–45. 5¼ inches high.

87. Three relief-moulded Staffordshire salt-glazed teawares of the 1740s. Attributed to Thomas & John Wedgwood of the Big House Pottery at Burslem. Covered jug, 6 inches high.

88. A superb and rare pair of moulded Staffordshire salt-glazed candlesticks. *c.* 1760. 9¼ inches high.

89. An ornately moulded Staffordshire salt-glazed jug of octagonal form. The panels including Adam and Eve, figures, animals, armorial bearings, and the initials 'OB'. *c.* 1750. 7¾ inches high.

Opposite page

90. Two related Staffordshire salt-glazed coffee pots with relief-moulded sprigged motifs added to a turned body and showing different treatments for decorative effect. *c.* 1740–50. 9 inches high.

91. A drab coloured mug and teapot with white applied-reliefs (as Plate 90 right) handle and spout. The inside of the mug also has a white clay-wash. These two colour pieces are attractive but quite simple to produce. *c.* 1740–50. Mug 5¼ inches high.

92. An attractive Staffordshire salt-glazed jug, with contrasting relief-motifs. *c.* 1740–50. 4⅜ inches high.

93. A pair of Staffordshire moulded salt-glazed sheep groups. *c.* 1750. 3¼ inches high.

94. A rare salt-glazed bear jug, the separate head forming a cup, the shredded clay simulating fur. *c.* 1740. 7 inches high.

95. A sharply moulded salt-glazed large plate or dish, of a typical type, made with several variations and produced in large quantities and exported to Europe and North America. *c.* 1750. Diameter 9¼ inches.

96. An attractive enamelled salt-glazed jug. *c.* 1755. 7¼ inches high.

97. A dumpy Staffordshire salt-glazed enamelled teapot. *c.* 1755. 5¼ inches high.

98. An imposing and rare double-handled loving-cup enamelled in the Oriental famille-rose style. *c.* 1750. 10 inches high.

99. A charming small-sized Staffordshire salt-glazed teapot, enamelled in the Chinese manner. *c.* 1755. 4¼ inches high.

100. A charmingly simple salt-glazed 'Ale' jug with scratched-blue decoration. Dated 1751. 7 inches high.

Following page
101. A rare scratched-blue-decorated salt-glazed loving-cup. Dated 1754, the initials E B perhaps relating to the Tunstal potter Enoch Booth. $7\frac{1}{4}$ inches high.

102. Two rare, moulded-edged salt-glazed plates bearing three-colour-printed decoration—perhaps applied at Liverpool or in London. *c.* 1750. Diameter $8\frac{1}{2}$ and 9 inches.

103. Three rare salt-glazed plates bearing printed designs, perhaps added at Liverpool or in London. Except for the centre Anti-Gallican Society example, the other two prints are also recorded on Chinese porcelains decorated in England. *c.* 1750. Diameter 7½ inches.

104. A well-enamelled Staffordshire salt-glazed bowl in the style of the popular Chinese porcelains. *c.* 1760. Diameter 7¾ inches.

105. Two very rare relief-moulded tiles, reputedly from Thomas Whieldon's house at Fenton Vivian. *c.* 1740. Diameter $4\frac{3}{4}$ inches.

106. A charmingly enamelled small-sized Staffordshire salt-glazed teapot. *c.* 1755–60. $4\frac{1}{2}$ inches high.

107. A rare dated small-sized Staffordshire salt-glazed teapot, painted with a representation of Bonnie Prince Charlie and inscribed 'Hannah Milns. 1759. Augt. 17th.' 4½ inches high.

108. A very rare form of Staffordshire salt-glazed, footed bowl, dated 1767. Diameter 8½ inches.

Veined Wares

The veined, or variegated, wares sometimes known as 'Agate' are very attractive. Most examples originate from the Staffordshire Potteries and fall within the 1710–1750 period, although the rare seventeenth-century stonewares made by Dwight (page 53) and Francis Place are of this general type.

From a potter's point of view these wares have great advantages. The decorative effect is achieved purely by 'wedging' together two, three, or more different coloured (or specially stained) clays. This simple process comprises laying thin 'bats' of different coloured clay one upon the other, alternately, until a convenient-sized block has been built. One then cuts through the mass with a wire-pull, placing the cut-off portion at a different angle on the top. This simple 'wedging' process is continued until a pleasing veined or variegated mix is formed. This mixed multi-coloured clay can then be worked in the normal way—turned on the wheel, or pressed into moulds. The great advantage is that no further decoration is required, and once the piece has been glazed and fired, no further firings are needed to fix the decoration.

The resulting wares are pleasing and novel, and the design is quite permanent. Objects such as knife-handles (Plate 109) lend themselves to this technique. In the clay numerous designs can be introduced—a geometric pattern is apparent in the fine teapot in Plate 111, left. The strange teapot with let-in sides, shown in Plate 115, has been built-up from thin bats of prepared clay.

A rather similar effect can be introduced by 'marbling', but here different coloured 'slips' are applied to a plain earthenware body, the slip being then worked together to form a marble-like effect. The covered tankard shown in Plate 114 is a typical example of this technique—one continued into the nineteenth century.

The early eighteenth-century Staffordshire veined or variegated wares are now rarely found perfect. Wedgwood was to use the same technique in the production of his classical, formed vases, later in the century; see Plates 146–47.

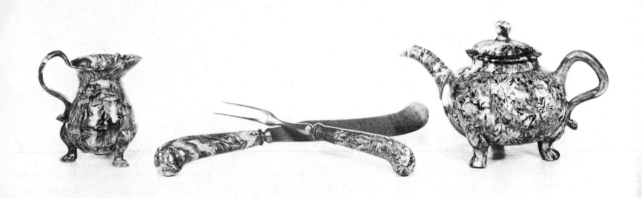

109. A Staffordshire solid agate-ware teapot, a creamer and two handles, in styles typical of the 1740s. Teapot $3\frac{1}{2}$ inches high.

110. An attractive and typical solid agate-ware creamer, with mask and claw feet—after silver prototypes. *c.* 1740. $3\frac{1}{4}$ inches high.

111. A very unusual solid agate-
ware teapot (left), the clay wedged
into a geometric design; contrasting with the more normal styles
shown to the right. *c.* 1740–45.
Left-hand teapot 5¾ inches high.

112. A solid agate-ware jug, the
rim dipped in white slip and of a
type attributed to Newcastle-under-
Lyme. *c.* 1745. 7½ inches high.

113. A noble solid agate-ware-covered jug, with side-handle, with lion knob. *c.* 1750. 10½ inches high.

114. A creamware-covered tankard, the surface decorated with a 'marbled' covering slip, in contrast to the earlier solid agate-type body. *c.* 1785. 7¾ inches high.

115. A primitive-looking solid agate teapot, mainly formed from separate sheets or 'bats' of prepared clay—rather as a carpenter would seek to form such a piece. 5 inches high.

Red-wares

The red-wares or 'Elers' wares were made, mainly within the Staffordshire Potteries, in imitation of the popular Oriental examples imported by the English East India Company. The English copies (examples were also made on the Continent) normally comprise teapots for which the unglazed body was much favoured, but coffee (Plate 119) or chocolate pots and other wares were also made.

The wares were formed mainly from moulds, which were also used for other bodies, a factory wasters show (Plate 116). It should be mentioned that many red-ware wasters were found on the Whieldon factory site, but the body was widely used, for from the potter's point of view these wares were reasonably trouble-free and inexpensive to produce. They do, at the same time, display good-quality workmanship, and many of the applied, 'sprigged' relief-motifs are quite charming (Plates 118–19). The red-wares are normally left unglazed, but some examples, often the later pieces, are glazed.

While the examples shown here have been given eighteenth-century dates, the ware was introduced in the later part of the seventeenth century. An intriguing advertisement for 'fine red, figured and flowered tea pots, chocolate cups' to be sold by auction, appeared in the *London Gazette* in February 1695, but we cannot now tell if these were Oriental examples or English copies. Certainly, however, the Dutch-born Elers brothers were making similar wares in London in the 1693 period and slightly later in Staffordshire. Dwight's 1684 Patent also covered 'opaceous red and dark coloured porcelaine or china', a ware which may equate with our red-wares.

A very good and well-illustrated account of the English red-wares is contained in two papers by Robin Price in the *Transactions of the English Ceramic Circle*, vol. 4, part 5, 1959, and vol. 5, part 3, 1962. An earlier paper by W. B. Honey in the *E.C.C. Transactions* No. 2 (1934) remains the classic account of the early red-wares and the work of the Elers.

116. A fine moulded Staffordshire red-ware teapot shown with matching wasters from Thomas Whieldon's factory-site at Fenton Vivian. *c.* 1730.

117. A fine Staffordshire, pierced-red-ware teapot, after a Chinese original. *c.* 1730–40. 5⅝ inches high.

119. An unusual Staffordshire red ware coffee pot with simple applied or sprigged decoration *c.* 1750–55. $8\frac{1}{4}$ inches high.

118. A typical Staffordshire red ware teapot of the 1740s or 50s, with applied motifs. $5\frac{1}{2}$ inches high.

Whieldon-type Wares

Although Thomas Whieldon, the famous Staffordshire potter, made all types of ware in general production in the eighteenth century (see paper by A. T. Morley Hewitt, *Transactions of the English Ceramic Circle*, vol. 3, part 3, 1954), his name is mainly associated with moulded and other wares coloured by means of wonderful semi-translucent coloured glazes—often applied in a mottled effect. While Whieldon undoubtedly made this type of glazed-pottery, he was by no means the only potter to do so and the term Whieldon-ware is best considered as a generic one.

Unfortunately, as with other basic types of ware, the makers did not employ identifying name-marks and without the evidence of documentary wasters from known and undisturbed factory-sites one cannot accurately identify the products of individual potters.

The attractive teapot shown in Plate 125 illustrates well the point that moulds were used for red-wares (see the previous section) and also for the Whieldon-glazed wares, for here we see Whieldon-factory waster covers in both basic bodies. The carved Chinese-style teapot shown in Plate 120 is seen in the unglazed red-ware body in Plate 117. Other moulds were pressed into service for salt-glazed stoneware as well as for the Whieldon-type earthen-wares, the relief mould 'King of Prussia' plate design (Plate 127) being a case in point.

The cauliflower tea and coffee wares (as Plates 126 and 128) proved very popular, and such wares were still being made in the nineteenth century. The pineapple teapot shown in Plate 129 is a rarer design in the same basic technique and style; here the waster cover is from the Whieldon factory-site. Mr Arnold Mountford's paper 'Thomas Whieldon's Manufactory at Fenton Vivian', contained in the *Transactions of the English Ceramic Circle*, vol. 8, part 2, 1972, is a valuable and interesting contribution to our knowledge of this potter's work.

The clear and warm semi-translucent coloured glazes were also applied to figures and groups, noticeably (but not exclusively) to those made by the elder Ralph Woods. The early toby-jugs were also decorated in this style before the duller overglaze enamel colours came into being in about 1790. Typical Ralph Wood-type figures are shown in Colour Plate V and in Plates 130–34. As yet no specialist book deals with the Whieldon wares but F. Falkner's magnificent book *The Wood Family of Burslem* (Chapman & Hall, London, 1912) covers the coloured-glazed figures and groups. Also of help we have Capt. R. K. Price's book *Astbury, Whieldon and Ralph Wood Figures and Toby Jugs* (John Lane, The Bodley Head, London, 1922).

120. A rare and unusual Whieldon-type tortoise-shell-glazed earthenware teapot. Of the same design as the red-ware pot shown in Plate 117. *c.* 1750. 5⅝ inches high.

121. A small and unusual relief-decorated Staffordshire tortoise-shell-glazed teapot. *c.* 1755. 4 inches high.

122. A rare moulded Flora tea-caddy and an ornate similar cornucopia-shaped wall-pocket, with tortoise-shell-type glaze effects. *c.* 1755. Wall-pocket $11\frac{3}{4}$ inches high.

123. A rare and attractive, moulded Staffordshire teapot, decorated with tortoise-shell-type glaze-effects. *c.* 1755–60. $4\frac{3}{4}$ inches high.

124. A simple and attractive, moulded Staffordshire teapot, the tinted semi-translucent glaze serving to accentuate the design. *c.* 1760. 5 inches high.

125. A fine, moulded Chinese-style teapot, the coloured glaze serving to enhance the raised design. Also shown are a red-ware cover and an earthenware lid waster from the Whieldon factory-site at Fenton Vivian. *c.* 1750–55.

126. A fine, relief-moulded cauliflower-patterned coffee pot. A popular design made by several potters over many years—reproductions occur. *c.* 1760. 8 inches high.

127. A rare, relief-moulded Staffordshire plate, decorated with tortoise-shell-type glaze-effect. The inscription reads 'Success to the King of Prussia and his Forces', a popular sentiment. This plate design also occurs in white salt-glaze. *c.* 1760. Diameter $9\frac{1}{4}$ inches.

128. A cauliflower-design moulded coffee pot, the leaf parts being washed with a semi-translucent green glaze. See also Plate 126. *c.* 1760. $9\frac{1}{2}$ inches high.

129. A rare, pineapple-design moulded Staffordshire teapot, decorated with semi-translucent green glaze in appropriate parts. The matching waster cover was found on the Whieldon site. *c.* 1755.

130. Two fine-quality Ralph Wood figures, attractively decorated with typical semi-translucent coloured glazes. Impressed mark Rª Wood with the model number 89. *c.* 1760. 11 and 9½ inches high.

131. Three fine Ralph Wood classical-style figures, enhanced with light, semi-translucent coloured glazes—in a typical manner. Models 21, 25, and 22 in the Ralph Wood list of models. *c.* 1765. Central Apollo figure 11¼ inches high.

Colour Plate V. A selection of Staffordshire Ralph Wood earthenwares of the 1770–90 period, showing the typical 18th-century semi-translucent coloured glazes. Toby-jug 11 inches high.

132. Three typical Ralph Wood-type toby-jugs, decorated with typical semi-translucent coloured glazes. Toby-jugs of this general type have been made from the middle of the 18th century to the present time. From about 1795 the enamel colours tend to be opaque rather than translucent. *c.* 1760. 9½ to 10¼ inches high.

133. A selection of moulded Staffordshire earthenware animal models of mid-18th-century date, simply decorated in an originally inexpensive style. Bear figure centre 2 inches high.

134. A selection of moulded Staffordshire earthenware figures decorated in a rather more ornate style than those shown above and of slightly later date *c.* 1770–80. Cat figure, centre, $2\frac{1}{8}$ inches high.

Sussex Wares

Although most basic types of pottery and ceramic decoration were widely produced at the various ceramic centres, there were some purely regional styles, produced at relatively small potteries mainly concerned with the manufacture of very utilitarian wares—baking or stewing-pots, flower-pots, or even bricks. On occasions these potters turned their attention to more decorative wares and to the manufacture of special, inscribed, objects. It is these special pieces which have been preserved while the main part of the potter's output has been lost.

Of these regional wares the Sussex wares are interesting and seem unique in the manner of their decoration. Into the dark, iron tinged, Sussex clay was pressed a metal die such as a printer would use. The resulting impression was then filled with a lighter contrasting clay to accentuate the motif. The whole was glazed and fired and no further decoration was required. Plates 135–37 show typical documentary examples illustrating the simple technique.

A good selection is preserved in the Hastings Museum. The curator, Mr J. Manwaring Baines, is an expert on the subject and the author of an interesting booklet. Other examples are to be found in other Sussex museums, including Worthing.

The reader is warned that some reproductions of Sussex wares were made in the present century but these lack the charm of the originals, and sometimes bear the Dicker Pottery mark.

135. A small Sussex-ware flask, the inlaid decoration being of a typical type. Note the printer's ampersand device repeated round the top edge. Dated 1792. 5¼ inches high.

136. A rare Sussex-ware tea-caddy, the inlaid inscription reading 'S & M Thomas, Rye Sussex. May 16 1808'. Note typical inlaid motifs— see also Plate 135. 5¾ inches high.

137. A documentary Sussex-ware flask with inlaid decoration, the impressions formed with printer's type and then filled with white or light-coloured clay. 1836. $5\frac{1}{4}$ inches high.

Wedgwood

While in the arrangement of this book the emphasis has been placed on the types of pottery rather than on individual makers, it is quite impossible to prepare a comprehensive work on British pottery without including a section on Josiah Wedgwood and the firm founded by this master potter. Here we have a token selection; other Wedgwood pieces are illustrated in subsequent general sections of this book. Any selection of illustrations even in a specialist book on this one factory can be merely a token, for the array of different bodies, shapes, and styles of decoration is seemingly endless, with one common denominator—quality.

The world-wide repute of the Wedgwood wares is highly deserved. Josiah set a standard of excellence that has never been equalled in pottery, a standard not confined to the potting and finish of the piece, but applying also to its design and decoration. This holds good not only for costly ornamental vases and the like but also for his humble wares—an everyday dinner plate in creamware or even his dairy equipment.

In many ways Josiah Wedgwood (1730–95) was a perfectionist, not only in the normal meaning of the word but in that he perfected existing standard wares. The cream-coloured earthenware body was in being long before Wedgwood refined it and gave it the imposing name 'Queen's Ware'. Similarly his 'basalt' ware was adapted from the standard 'Egyptian black' body (see page 151). While others were seeking to cut corners to lower costs, Wedgwood strove for perfection and having achieved it he sought to find, or to make, a market for his wares.

Here too he was a far-sighted businessman, going to great lengths (and expense) to get his products placed in society and so talked about and publicised. He did not believe in reducing prices but rather to add to the standing of his pieces by charging a relatively high price. Rather than be fettered by the china dealers of the day, he established his own showrooms in London, showrooms that were to become the meeting place of fashionable society.

Success came, but it did not arrive overnight, it was the result of painstaking research and labour. In 1754, reputedly at the age of fourteen, Josiah Wedgwood entered in a partnership with Thomas Whieldon, the famous potter (see page 98), but five years later he started potting on his own account at the Ivy House Works, Burslem, moving in 1764 to the large Brick House Works also known as the Bell Works. Here the useful wares were made until 1773, although the ornamental objects had been made at the specially built Etruria factory from its opening on 13 June 1769 (see Plates 139–40).

The early unmarked wares made before about 1760 are extremely difficult to attribute with certainty and in this general review the range shown is restricted to the later pieces— those that bear a clear name-mark. It is a fair rule of thumb that if a piece does not bear a Wedgwood name-mark it is not Wedgwood, but there are exceptions and important ones too. The original issue of the famous Portland vase does not bear a mark (the base is shown in Plate 138), nor does the famous anti-slavery medallion. Nevertheless, useful wares from at

110

138. The base or underside of one of Wedgwood's original copies of the famous Portland vase (see Plate 154). These early examples are unmarked.

ast 1800 onwards should bear one of the standard marks listed at the end of this outline ccount.

While Wedgwood is best remembered for his ornamental wares in two-colour jasper— or his blue vases and the like with white relief motifs, it is perhaps for his relatively humble, parsely decorated table wares in a refined cream-coloured earthenware, later termed 'Queen's Vare', that he should be remembered. This light, clean-looking ware established his overseas narkets and largely replaced the traditional Continental tin-glazed earthenwares. Much of the arly Wedgwood creamware was sent to Sadler of Liverpool to be embellished with overglaze rints. Examples of this work are shown in Plates 182–83 and 301, and the overall story of cream-coloured earthenware is told in a separate section, on page 140.

The golden period of Wedgwood pottery was surely that known as 'Wedgwood & Bentley' (*c.* 1768–80), when noble ornamental wares were made under the joint names of osiah Wedgwood and his non-potting partner, Thomas Bentley. (The useful wares con- inued to be made under Wedgwood's sole account although some decorative teapots and ugs have the Wedgwood & Bentley mark.) For design and potting skill the Wedgwood & Bentley wares of the 1768–80 period stand alone. Representative marked specimens are hown here in Plates 141–43, 145, 147–51. In December 1781, after Bentley's death in November 1780, the stock of the Wedgwood & Bentley partnership was sold at auction by

British Pottery

Mr Christie. This catalogue comprising some twelve hundred lots is preserved in th
archives of the present firm—Messrs Christie, Manson & Woods. Brief extracts from th
historic sale catalogue are of interest since they show the range of these relatively earl
decorative pieces, but, to quote from the catalogue, 'the table and dessert services etc., i
Queens Ware, being the Property of Mr. Wedgwood alone, are not included in this sale bu
continue to be sold at his rooms in Greek Street, Soho, as usual. . . .'

The Wedgwood & Bentley decorative wares, in which Thomas Bentley's widow had a
interest, included 'Cameos, intaglios, bas-reliefs, medallions, busts, vases, statues, animal
candelabra, bouquetiers, ecritoires, garden pots, &c. &c.', and it is interesting to note that b
1781 Wedgwood was able to claim: 'The nature and quality of the ornaments made b
Wedgwood & Bentley are generally known throughout Europe. . . .' The catalogue contain
descriptions of the bodies then in production—'basaltes, Jasper, white porcelain [not a tru
porcelain as we use the description today], terra cotta, and imitations of Porphyry, Pebbl
and other stones and encaustic paintings from the ancient Etruscan vases and the fines
Grecian Gems'.

I cannot resist quoting a few items from this 1781 catalogue, with the prices the
realised.

A set of five Etruscan painted basalt vases, subjects a fine group of female
figures, triumphal sacrifice and canopi with symobals, serving for
candelabra. £1 15

A set of seven such vases sold for £4 14

Twelve (basalt) teapots (Plate 198), two sugar dishes, two cream buckets, one
tea cannister, one coffee pot with Etruscan borders in encaustic painting,
one cup and two bread and butter plates, with ditto. £1 2

A suite of three encaustic paintings for pictures, Diomede, Dog and Eagle
from Maffie's Gems. £1 6

Two large basalt busts, the two De Witts. £2 10

A suite of seven, chimney ornaments,—one statue of Apollo, two busts of
Shakespeare and Garrick, two boys from Fiamingo and two triton
candelabra. £2 9

A suite of sixty medallions for a cabinet, the Roman history. . . . £1 3

A suite of two hundred in a mahogany cabinet; Kings and Queens of Asia
Minor and of Greece, Statesmen, Philosophers. . . . £8 0

Twelve intaglios set in gilt material and twelve ditto, with a catalogue. 17

A set of five ornamental vases, in imitation of Granite, the two end vases
serving for candelabra (Plate 145). £2 11

A set of five ornamental vases, in imitation of Agate, the end vases with gold
burnt in and burnished. £1 2

A pair of jasper bracelets set in gold . . . two neck pins in gold, . . . one gold
locket, a gold ring set Isis and a gold seal, set King and Queen. £4 12

112

I have quoted but twelve of twelve hundred lots, but enough to make the mouth water and to show the range of the pre-1781 Wedgwood & Bentley products. However, the end of the Wedgwood & Bentley period did not mean a drastic change in policy, in the Wedgwood designs or in the quality of the wares, for Wedgwood himself was still in charge. The charming encaustic-painted basalt teapot shown in Plate 153 could well be Wedgwood & Bentley but it bears the post-1780 'Wedgwood' mark. This mark is, however, interesting and early and is that known as 'upper and lower case', with a capital letter W and the remaining letters being in lower case, as can be clearly seen in Plate 152. This upper-and-lower-case mark was used during the 1780–98 period and subsequent Wedgwood marks have the letters of a uniform size. The quality of the pre-1800 Wedgwood ware is evidenced by the first copies of the famous Portland vase; a side-view is shown in Plate 154, although no photograph can do justice to the thin clear-cut reliefs on this first issue of the 1790–95 period. Note especially the finely 'tooled' mask-head and the three-dimensional effect seen in the crossed legs and feet of the seated figure. The Portland vase was, however, reproduced several times in the nineteenth century—often in 'Wedgwood blue' rather than in the near-black of the original and several other firms produced very inferior versions.

Mention of 'Wedgwood blue' (a colour description that has passed into the English language) leads naturally to Wedgwood's 'jasper' body. This is a subject which deserves, and has been given, a separate section (see page 174), but it should be stated here that Wedgwood introduced this body in 1774 when he described the result of his lengthy experiments in the following words—

> A white porcelain bisque of exquisite beauty and delicacy, possessing the general qualities of the Basaltes together with that of receiving colours through its whole substance, in a manner which no other body, ancient or modern, has been known to do.

The Portland vase is of this jasper body (Plate 154), as are thousands upon thousands of other Wedgwood products, ranging from huge vases to minute medallions for mounting in jewellery. Some of the many colours to which this body could be tinted are to be seen in Colour Plate XIV of the *Illustrated Encyclopaedia of British Pottery and Porcelain* (Herbert Jenkins, London, 1966). The body has remained in continuous production up to the present time, for some two hundred years. The commonest colours are light blue or a dark blue and the later, post-1860 examples are not particularly rare, especially the standard shapes of tea wares, although some pieces can be of a very good standard and several shapes or objects are rare and well worth the attention of collectors.

Progressing into the nineteenth century we have a bewildering range of Wedgwood wares to mention. The rare and collectable variegated 'moonlight-lustre' effect is seen in Plate 155, while the teapot illustrated in Plate 156 is of an uncommon form and has blue-jasper reliefs on a white ground. The tastefully designed creamware shapes and the characteristic restrained decoration found on such table wares is typified in Plate 157, while the broad subject of creamware is featured on page 140. An attractive shell-motif dessert service is shown in Plate 158 and these popular forms were produced over a lengthy period from about 1820 onwards.

Among the less expensive Wedgwood wares we must single out the moulded green-glazed wares (Plate 159). Here the semi-translucent glaze was flooded over the moulded design, the glaze serving to accentuate the pattern by darkening the indented parts because of the thickness of glaze retained therein. Very many firms produced such pieces but none approach in quality the Wedgwood examples, although some slight differences of glaze colour must be expected between the different pieces in a large service, owing to some pieces taking up more glaze than others.

In the nineteenth century quantities of basalt ware were produced, relying for its decorative merits on the relief-motifs, but early in the present century a range of very fine pieces was produced with gold embellishments. One such example is illustrated in Plate 160. Further Wedgwood wares are featured in subsequent sections of this book, in Plates 183, 187, 189, 191–92, 198–203, 226–40, 245, 364, 533–34, 541–44, 549, 604–7, and Colour Plate VIII.

The basic Wedgwood marks are fairly simple. The standard mark is the word 'WEDG-WOOD' impressed. A very rare version used in the 1760s has unevenly placed letters, each one being seemingly impressed into the body separately. From *c.* 1780 to 1798 the name appears in upper- and lower-case letters—as shown in Plate 152. The joint names 'Wedgwood & Bentley' occur on *ornamental* wares during the 1769–80 period, and on very small objects the initials 'W & B' were used. The word 'ETRURIA' occurs with the Wedgwood name in the 1840s, and the description 'Wedgwood's Stone China' occurs on this Ironstone-type body during the 1827–61 period. A system of recording the month and year of manufacture by means of a series of three impressed letters was introduced in 1860 but these letters do not appear on all wares and they should not be confused with the single letter, which can appear under the standard Wedgwood name-mark at an earlier date. Full details of the three-letter dating system and of the later marks are given in my *Encyclopaedia of British Pottery and Porcelain Marks* (Herbert Jenkins, London, 1964) but it should be remembered that if the word 'England' appears the piece was made after 1891 and if 'Made in England' occurs the specimen will have been made after about 1910. The place-name 'Barlaston', the home of the present factory, denotes a post-1940 dating.

The serious collector of Wedgwood has at his disposal a baffling array of reference-books, some of which are listed below, but he would be well advised to join one of the specialist clubs, the officers and members of which will give most valuable advice and help. The English Society is called simply The Wedgwood Society (Hon. Sec. Mrs B. Jarvis, The Roman Villa, Rockbourne, Fordingbridge, Hants) and its Transactions are invaluable for their learned papers and candid book reviews! Most museums display a fair selection of Wedgwood ware, notably the Victoria & Albert Museum in London. The Wedgwood's Works Museum is also of great interest and a tour of the factory is to be recommended to any collector. The finest collection of Wedgwood, however, is to be seen in America, at the Buten Museum of Wedgwood, Merion, Pennsylvania. The late Harry M. Buten was a most enthusiastic collector and the author of several books—particularly on the unusual aspects of Wedgwood.

Apart from the following standard books on the Wedgwood wares, the collector will benefit greatly from an understanding of the man and the period in which he lived. Here his letters are of the utmost interest and works such as *The Selected Letters of Josiah Wedgwood* by A. Finer and G. Savage (Cory, Adams & Mackay, London, 1965) are revealing. Miss Meteyard's two-volume *Life of Josiah Wedgwood*, published by Hurst & Blackett of London in 1865, is likewise full of background information. Among the standard works the reader will find the following of assistance.

Wedgwood Ware by W. B. Honey (Faber & Faber, London, 1948).
Wedgwood by W. Mankowitz (E. P. Dutton, New York, 1953).
Decorative Wedgwood in Architecture & Furniture by A. Kelly (Country Life, London, 1965).
Wedgwood Ware by A. Kelly (Ward Lock, London, 1970).
Wedgwood Jasper by R. Reilly (Charles Letts, London, 1972).
Wedgwood: the portrait medallions by R. Reilly & G. Savage (Barrie & Jenkins, London, 1973).

Publicity booklets published by Messrs Wedgwood are also helpful and the photographs of museum exhibits in *Wedgwood Museum Barlaston* (1969) are of a very high standard.

Some light on the early unmarked wares is contained in the paper 'William Greatbatch and the Early Wedgwood Wares' by D. Towner, published in the *Transactions of the English Ceramic Circle*, vol. 5, part 4, 1963.

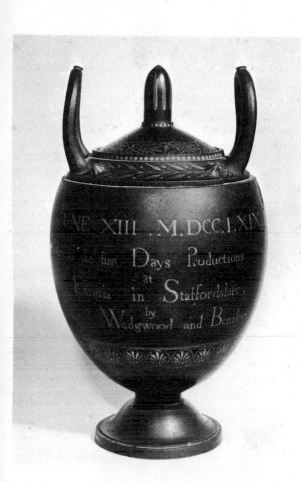

139. The front view of a Wedgwood & Bentley basalt vase, one made to commemorate the first day's production at the new Etruria works and decorated in the so-called Etruscan manner. 1769. 10 inches high.

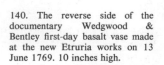

140. The reverse side of the documentary Wedgwood & Bentley first-day basalt vase made at the new Etruria works on 13 June 1769. 10 inches high.

141. A tasteful Wedgwood & Bentley basalt vase of large size. Relief-moulded circular mark, *c.* 1770–80. 15¼ inches high.

142. A rare and fine-quality marked Wedgwood & Bentley basalt vase. *c.* 1770–80. 14 inches high.

143. A pair of Wedgwood & Bentley (relief-moulded circular mark) vases, the body coloured to emulate stone. Basalt plinths. *c.* 1770–80. 9½ inches high.

144. One of a pair of Wedgwood creamware (Queen's Ware) bulb-pots with pierced covers, the body coloured to emulate stone. Traces of the original gilding on the relief work. Impressed marked 'Wedgwood'. *c.* 1785. 9⅝ inches long.

145. An extremely rare Wedgwood & Bentley cassolette-vase, the multi-purpose cover reversible to act as a candle-holder (as shown) or merely as an ornamental knob (on the other side). The relief-work and handles retain most of the original gilding. Basalt plinth. Circular relief-moulded name-mark. $13\frac{3}{4}$ inches high. *c.* 1770–80.

146. A rare and superb garniture of fine Wedgwood & Bentley transitional mantle vases (cover of centre vase missing), the cream-ware bodies coloured to emulate natural stone. Traces of original gilding on relief-work. Circular relief-moulded Wedgwood & Bentley marks, also on some the single word 'Wedgwood'. Centre vase 13 inches high. *c.* 1780–85.

147. A Wedgwood & Bentley (relief-moulded circular mark) vase of typical type emulating natural stone. *c.* 1770–80. 11 inches high.

148. A graceful Wedgwood & Bentley (relief-moulded circular mark) vase with elegant relief-motifs contrasting with the tinted variegated ground. *c.* 1770–80. 18½ inches high.

149. A marked Wedgwood & Bentley basalt bust, a fine-quality example typical of the 1770—80 period. 16 inches high.

150. A fine and rare, marked Wedgwood & Bentley, plaque depicting The Apotheosis of Homer, by Flaxman. *c.* 1770—80. $7\frac{1}{2} \times 14\frac{1}{2}$ inches.

Colour Plate XI. A fine, oval-footed comport showing the lush quality of many of Pratt's multicolour printed earthenwares. The printed centre is 'Highland Music' after Sir Edwin Landseer, and bears the Pratt's engraver's signature 'J Austin Sc'. The printed acorn and oak-leaf border is one of Pratt's basic borders on these fine table wares; it can be plain or embellished with gilding. *c.* 1851. $12\frac{1}{2}$ inches long.

151. The front and reverse of typical Wedgwood & Bentley oval basalt portrait plaques. The reversed example showing the impressed name—often abbreviated to 'W & B' on small objects. *c.* 1770–80. $2\frac{3}{4} \times 2\frac{1}{4}$ inches.

152. An early version of the impressed Wedgwood name-mark, incorporating upper- and lower-case letters. The number 2 refers to the size (of the teapot shown below), or is sometimes a potter's tally-mark. *c.* 1780–85.

153. A fine-quality Wedgwood basalt teapot tastefully enhanced with encaustic enamels in the Antique style. Mark as Plate 152 above. *c.* 1780–85. 7½ inches long.

Opposite page

154. A side-view of the famous Portland vase. This example is one of the first issue, and the finely moulded and tooled-up mask and the thin leaves below should be noted. In some later issues, post-1839, the male figure is partly clothed. See also Plate 138. *c.* 1790–95. 10 inches high.

55. A Wedgwood creamware flower-bowl of Antique form (found in several different bodies and decorative styles) decorated in the so-called variegated moonlight lustre. Impressed name-mark. *c.* 1810. 8 inches long.

56. A white jasper teapot, decorated with blue relief-motifs, a simple but attractive design. *c.* 1820. 8¾ inches long.

Opposite page
57. A Wedgwood creamware dessert service, finely potted and enamelled in a typical restrained style. The crest is an unusual feature and most sets had only a simple border. *c.* 1805. Ice-pail 8 inches high.

Previous pages

158. Representative pieces from a Wedgwood pearl-ware dessert service showing typical marine forms. These shapes were introduced early in the 19th century and are still popular. They occur in several different bodies and styles of decoration. *c.* 1820. Centrepiece 9 inches high.

159. Representative pieces from a relief-moulded Victorian dessert set. The moulded design being accentuated by the green glaze, showing darker according to the thickness of glaze—dark in the recessed parts of the design. This simple technique was extremely effective, cheap, and popular. Wedgwood made several such designs—as did most of the 19th-century firms. *c.* 1850–60. Centrepiece 12½ inches long.

160. A Wedgwood basalt ewer, after a Flaxman design. A popular model, here enriched with gilding in a style popular early in the present century. Impressed namemark with gilt pattern-number Z 3618. 15 inches high.

Wedgwood-styled Wares

If imitation be the sincerest form of flattery, then Josiah Wedgwood must be the most flattered of potters, for countless English and Continental firms emulated in various degrees the Wedgwood styles. These imitations fall into two categories, those bearing the true name-mark of their maker and those which we can fairly regard as fakes, rather than imitations, in that they bear a copy, or near copy, of the Wedgwood name-mark.

Some of Wedgwood's eighteenth-century contempories produced superb quality wares, sometimes equalling the finish of the master and being in most cases rarer than the true Wedgwood examples. The rare marked 'Palmer' vase shown in Plate 161, shows the taste and finish of some imitations. Another of Wedgwood's great competitors was James Neale of the Church Works at Hanley and characteristic examples are shown in Plates 162–64. Other good basalt wares are shown in Plates 193–97, 204–23.

Many firms produced the ever-popular Jasper wares. Here we see examples from the famous Spode firm (Plate 166) and a 'Steel'-marked watch-stand (Plate 165) representing the host of smaller, almost unknown, Staffordshire potters. Other Wedgwood-type Jasper wares are shown in Plates 241–44. The two marked 'E. Mayer' cane-ware ewers shown in Plate 167 illustrate well the quality of the wares made by this Hanley potter in the 1790–1804 period. The moulded green-glazed marked 'Stevenson' plate illustrated in Plate 168 represents the many manufacturers of this type of ware, for which Wedgwood was famous over so long a period.

Next we should consider the fake Wedgwood wares or those bearing a mark easily mistaken for the standard Wedgwood mark. We have, for example, fine creamwares such as the tureen shown in Plate 169, of a typical Wedgwood-shape and decorated with a typical border-design (an almost identical true Wedgwood tureen is shown in the *Illustrated Encyclopaedia of British Pottery and Porcelain*, Plate 607), but the impressed name-mark reads 'WIEGWOOD', a mark to be found on many other Wedgwood-styled wares.

The two 'Wedgwood'-marked creamware figures shown in Plate 170 are of a class that presents problems, they are obviously not true Wedgwood, on account of their poor finish and general lack of life! They could have been made especially for Wedgwood to fill an order (for much such intertrading took place between the Staffordshire potters), or they could be the product of Ralph Wedgwood (1766–1837), a potter at Burslem from 1785 to 1796 and later at Knottingley in Yorkshire. Here he traded as Tomlinson, Foster, Wedgwood & Co. but the partnership used the somewhat misleading mark 'Wedgwood & Co' until he left in January 1801. A Wedgwood & Co pattern book has been preserved and sample designs from it are reproduced by Heather Lawrence in *The Connoisseur* magazine, June 1974, and further information will be contained in that author's book *Pots and Potteries of Yorkshire* (David & Charles, 1975).

This same mark was also used by Wedgwood & Co. of Tunstall, Staffordshire from 1860 until 1965 when it was retitled 'Enoch Wedgwood (Tunstall) Ltd'. Although these

'Wedgwood & Co' marks have caused confusion, this should not occur for the tru
Wedgwood firm did not employ the additional '& Co', using only the single nam
'Wedgwood'.

John Wood of Burslem somewhat craftily took the middle name Wedge or Wedg
enabling him to use the name-mark WEDGWOOD with the slightest gap between the tw
words. Wood worked between 1841 and 1860, one of his printed plates is shown in Plat
172.

Away from Staffordshire several potters employed misleading Wedgwood-type mark
Some potters used the mark 'VEDGWOOD', one blue-printed platter by Carr & Patton o
North Shields is shown in Plate 173. One of Wedgwood's greatest copyists was the firm c
William Smith & Co., Stockton-on-Tees, and while their wares are not truly in th
Wedgwood-style (Plate 174), the marks were. Wedgwoods gained an injunction in 184
against their use of the marks Wedgwood or Wedgewood. This firm also used the descrip
tion 'Queens Ware' but normally the initials 'W. S. & Co.' are included to right in part th
flattery! William Smith & Co. are also believed to have used the name 'Vedgwood' on thei
products, which fall within the period 1825–55.

One should remember that the main Wedgwood firm used the simple name-mar
WEDGWOOD, without a middle E, without the initial J, and without the additiona
'& Co.'.

161. A superb Wedgwood &
Bentley-style creamware vase
emulating natural stone, the relief-
motifs gilt (now slightly worn) and
mounted on a basalt plinth. Circulr
relief-moulded mark 'H Palmer,
Hanley'. *c.* 1770–78. 10 inches
high.

162. A fine-quality pair of marked 'J Neale, Hanley' vases in the Wedgwood & Bentley style—emulating natural stone. *c.* 1770–78. 9½ inches high.

163. A rare garniture of three marked Neale of 'Hanly' (the 'e' is often missing in this place-name on Neale marks) in the style of Wedgwood & Bentley. The gilding on the creamware reliefs is somewhat worn. *c.* 1770–78. 12½ and 10 inches high.

164. A fine Neale of 'Hanly' (see Plate 163) basalt-ware vase, of the same basic form as the veined creamware examples shown in the preceding illustration. Cover missing. *c.* 1770–78. $10\frac{1}{4}$ inches high.

165. A rare blue and white Jasper watch-stand bearing the impressed mark 'Steel. Burslem'. *c.* 1810–24. 6¾ inches high.

166. A rare impressed marked 'Spode' three-colour Jasper flower-basket in the Wedgwood manner. *c.* 1810–20. 4¾ inches high.

167. A superb pair of marked
'E Mayer' dry-bodied cane-ware
cream-jugs in the Wedgwood style.
c. 1795–1804. 5 inches high.

168. A green-glazed relief-moulded
dessert plate in the Wedgwood-
style (see Plate 159) but marked
'Stevenson'. John Stevenson of
Shelton was one of the rarer
makers of this type of ware. *c.*
1850. Diameter 8¾ inches.

169. An almost exact copy of a Wedgwood creamware tureen of a standard shape and enamelled border-design (see *An Illustrated Encyclopaedia of British Pottery and Porcelain*, Plate 607) but bearing the rare, impressed mark 'WIEGWOOD', one of several employed that appear at first glance to read Wedgwood without infringing any rights. English *c.* 1810.

170. Two impressed marked 'Wedgwood' creamware figures, probably made by Ralph Wedgwood of Burslem in the 1790s, but not by the famous Josiah Wedgwood firm. Female figure 7 inches high.

171. A blue-printed plate showing the famous and much copied 'Asiatic Pheasants' design as made by Wedgwood & Co. of Tunstall. The main Wedgwood firm did not have the '& Co' incorporated in their marks. *c.* 1860–70.

172. A printed plate bearing the misleading mark J. Wedg Wood (with a slight gap between the two words) as shown in the *Encyclopaedia of British Pottery and Porcelain Marks*, number 4276 b. *c.* 1838–60.

173. A fine blue-printed platter bearing the impressed 'Vedgwood' mark, also the printed mark of Carr & Patton of the Low Lights Pottery at North Shields. Several, mainly North Country, potters seem to have employed the misleading 'Vedgwood' mark in the middle of the 19th century.

174. Two mid-19th-century earthenware plates bearing the impressed 'Vedgwood' mark, also 'W S & Co's Wedgewood' (note the middle 'e') relating to William Smith & Co. of Stockton-on-Tees. *c.* 1850.

Creamwares

The refined, whitish or cream-coloured earthenware now called 'Queen's Ware' made i[..] impact all over Europe. Its light weight and thin gauge coupled with the smooth lead-glaz[..] ensured that it ousted the old tin-glazed Delft and faience-type earthenwares. In England [..] also replaced the salt-glazed wares with their uneven and hard orange-skin-like glaze. It wa[..] the potter's answer to the expensive white porcelain body.

The introduction of the new cream-coloured lightweight body was, however, gradual. A[..] first the Staffordshire potters coated the surface of their dark-clay-coloured wares with [..] thin white slip, rather in the Delft tradition, but with the introduction of flint (calcined an[..] finely ground) and West Country clays into the body early in the eighteenth century, whi[..] wares became practical. When highly fired a stoneware body was produced, but when fire[..] to a moderate temperature and dipped in a lead glaze, the new cream-coloured war[..] resulted. It was introduced in about 1740, and by 1760 it was the standard English potter[..] body being produced, not merely in Staffordshire but in a host of out-potteries—that i[..] outside Staffordshire. The Leeds factory is noted for the quality of its creamware, but thi[..] Yorkshire factory is by no means a lone example. The original term employed for what w[..] now rather loosely call 'Queen's Ware', a term coined by Wedgwood in about 1767, wa[..] 'cream colour' or 'cream coloured' giving rise to the potters' abbreviation 'C C' to be foun[..] in old accounts and receipts.

The early, pre-1760 creamwares often show a marked similarity to the salt-glaze shape[..] and indeed many pieces were produced from the moulds formerly used to form the sal[..] glazed stonewares. Also the hand of some decorators can be traced on creamware as well a[..] salt-glaze. There can have been no fine demarcation line between the production of thes[..] bodies; one factory might be making salt-glazed stoneware while its neighbour had alread[..] changed to the new creamware. Or one factory might have made wares in both bodies. I[..] any case the creamware soon superseded all others. The lightweight wares with a relativel[..] non-chipping glaze were also easily transported and Wedgwood in particular (but by n[..] means exclusively) built-up a flourishing export-market.

The styles of decoration are various. Plain, relief-moulded, pieces (Plate 176) wer[..] inexpensive to produce. Some were painted in blue under the glaze in the popular Orienta[..] fashion (Plate 175). Much was repetitively decorated with the help of overglaze printin[..] (Plates 178, 180–83), while a large proportion of pieces were embellished with overglaz[..] enamels—in the manner of the porcelain decorators. In the eighteenth century th[..] enamelled designs tended to follow the porcelain fashions, but from the 1780s into th[..] nineteenth century the vogue for simple border-motifs came into fashion, so that the centre[..] of plates were unadorned (Plates 185, 187, 189, 190). Here we have utilitarian creamwar[..] at its best, neatly potted, tastefully decorated.

These simply decorated creamware (or perhaps 'pearl-ware') dinner services were quit[..] inexpensive—or they seem so by today's standards. In 1812 a London retailer wa[..]

dvertising hundred and eighty-three-piece dinner sets at £3.13.6 in plain creamware, 5.15.6. with a blue edging, or £6.16.6. with a green edge. Blue-printed sets in the Chinese yle were more expensive, £7.17.6. for nearly two hundred pieces!

The cream-coloured ware gave way in turn to pearl-ware, basically a whiter body, the hiteness accentuated by a slightly blued-glaze (Plate 186). This body was introduced by Tedgwood as early as 1779 but it did not come into general favour for some time. Tedgwood himself noted in a letter to his partner Thomas Bentley '. . . the pearl white must e considered as a change rather than an improvement. . . .' A most important article by or Noel-Hume is contained in the American magazine *Antiques* of March 1969. Here this arned author writes of pearl-ware as 'one of the landmarks in the evolution of English arthenware, providing a bridge between creamware . . . and the bone-china, ironstone, ranite and porcelaneous wares of the nineteenth century . . . .' Mr Noel-Hume also suggests aat the description 'china-glazed' earthenware found in so many Staffordshire directories om the 1780s into the nineteenth century, was the contemporary name for what we now all pearl-ware and if this is the case then these directories show that individual potters aade both creamware and pearl-ware, for example we find entries such as

'Wm Adams & Co. Cream-coloured ware and china glaze ware painted' (Tunnicliffe's 1787 directory).

o the layman it is often difficult to distinguish between the creamware body and the whiter earl-ware with its slightly blue-tinted 'china' glaze. The pearl-ware often feels more open nd porous but it seems likely that much English pearl-ware will continue to be confused ith better-known and respected creamware.

Most early, pre-1770 creamwares are unmarked, as are all too many later specimens and aeir attribution to any one maker, or even district, is often very uncertain. Popular names uch as 'Leeds' are bandied about with wild enthusiasm but the new collector can rely on Donald Towner's 1957 classic *English Cream-coloured Earthenware* (Faber & Faber, .ondon) to give a firm foundation to a large and complicated subject. Mr Towner's paper Some Cream Ware Comparisons' in the *Transactions of the English Ceramic Circle*, vol. 4, art 3, 1957, is also helpful.

176. An early, relief-moulded creamware teapot of rare form and undecorated in the salt-glaze tradition. *c.* 1760. 5¼ inches high.

Opposite page
175. A large and superb early creamware jug of Leeds type, painted in underglaze-blue in the Chinese manner and inscribed 'Patrick Ryon, 1776. Success to the Lickhill'. Of fine, lightweight body with a rich, glassy, creamy glaze. 11 inches high.

177. A rare, early Leeds-type creamware jug, enamelled in red and black. *c.* 1775. 8¼ inches high.

178. A rare Cockpit Hill Derby creamware teapot of characteristic shape. The printed design copied from a Russian coin of 1765. The front is shown as Plate 238 in *An Illustrated Encyclopaedia of British Pottery and Porcelain. c.* 1765–70. 5 inches high.

179. A rare Wedgwood creamware coffee pot enamelled (outside the factory) in shades of green. *c.* 1760. 9½ inches high.

180. A rare creamware plate, the central print (in red) includes the name 'Leeds Pottery'. *c.* 1775. Diameter 9½ inches.

181. A Staffordshire creamware plate, decorated with a superbly engraved scenic design. Unmarked but dated 1786. Similar examples, which are, perhaps, later replacements, bear the impressed mark 'Wedgwood & Co.' as used by Ralph Wedgwood & Co. of Burslem. Diameter 9¾ inches.

182. Unmarked creamwares, almost certainly of Wedgwood make, decorated by means of overglaze prints by Sadler of Liverpool with 'Liverpool bird' designs. Much Wedgwood creamware was sent to Liverpool to be printed. *c.* 1775.

183. An impressed marked 'Wedgwood' creamware tureen. The overglaze prints almost certainly added by Sadler of Liverpool. *c.* 1775. 8¼ inches high.

184. A fine relief-moulded cream ware jug, the design enriched wit semi-translucent, and also wit opaque, enamels. Incised dat under the base 1793. 8¼ inche high.

185. A simple Staffordshire cream-ware plate with enamelled border. Marked on reverse 'W.B. 1799'. Diameter 10 inches.

186. An attractive, brown-printed pearl-ware platter, from a dinner service, `bearing the impressed mark 'Wedgwood & Co'. Ralph Wedgwood of Burslem used this mark in the 1785–96 period. 10 × 7½ inches.

187. A rare, impressed marked
'Wedgwood' creamware honey-pot,
from a long dinner, dessert, and
breakfast service (see also Plate
189), with typical enamelled border. *c.* 1815. 5 inches high.

188. A fine-quality marked
'Wilson' creamware tureen from a
dessert service, showing characteristic moulded border. *c.* 1800. 6
inches high.

189. A rare Wedgwood creamware oval basket (with metal and wicker handle) and stand, from the same long set as Plate 187, one purchased in Holland. Much English creamware was exported. *c.* 1815. Stand $7\frac{3}{4} \times 6$ inches.

190. A small, impressed marked 'Turner' creamware tureen and stand, from a large service in the Wedgwood style. *c.* 1790–1800. 6 inches long.

Basalt

The ceramic term 'basalt' was coined by Josiah Wedgwood to describe a refined version of the standard unglazed black body known as 'Egyptian black'. Wedgwood in his 1787 catalogue described his ware as 'a black porcelain biscuit (that is unglazed body) of nearly the same properties with the natural stone, striking fire from steel, receiving a high polish, serving as a touchstone for metals, resisting all acids and bearing without injury a strong fire—stronger indeed than the basaltes itself'. The earlier standard 'Egyptian black' wares were in everyday use by the 1760s and were soon being exported, for the *New York Gazette* in 1762 carried an advertisement for English 'Egyptian black teapots, milk-pots, mugs and teabowls of all sizes'.

On the face of it the dull black body has little or no decorative potential, yet the British potters turned it into a standard commercial line, one that remained popular from at least 1760 well into the nineteenth century, and Messrs Wedgwood still produce today their basalt wares (Plate 604) for the home and export market, some two hundred years after its introduction.

The answer to its popularity is basically the quality of the potting and the design of the forms—especially of the earlier wares. Witness the quality of the tankard shown in Colour Plate VII, with its engine-turned fluted bands, the applied 'sprigged' festoons and other motifs. In this example we see also a very rare feature, the inlaid white border-design at the top and bottom edge.

The Wedgwood basalt wares of the Wedgwood & Bentley period, *c.* 1768–80, are particularly fine, they are of a compact body which takes a pleasing polish. The general quality of design and finish is also superb, qualities reflected in the price such pieces command. Wedgwood examples of this period are shown in Plates 191–92 (also in Plates 141–42, 149, and 151). It is noticeable that Wedgwood chose the basalt body with which to form his commemorative 'First-Day' vases when the famous Etruria factory was opened in June 1769 (see Plates 139–40). These vases were, however, over-painted in the so-called encaustic colours, most of these painted vases bear classical figure subjects (Plates 199, 201–3), while other pieces, often the table wares, bear only tasteful border-designs (Plates 198 and 200).

Wedgwood was by no means alone in producing good-quality basalt wares; nearly every Staffordshire potter made such wares, as did various others in our other main ceramic centres. Examples by Neale and by Palmer are shown in Plates 193–97. The Spode company also produced very fine quality basalt wares, and examples are shown in Plates 204–6. Typical pieces from a representative selection of other potteries are illustrated in Plates 207–13, 215–24.

While I tend to show marked specimens which can often be dated to narrow limits, it is true that most pieces are unmarked. Some of these unmarked examples can be very fine and are represented here by the engine-turned jug shown in Plate 214 with its slight silvery embellishments. Some unmarked pieces can, however, be approximately dated by reference to the subjects which can depict historical events, see Plate 225.

The purely English ceramic body must have been very popular with the potters, for the body was easy to prepare and to work. Most pieces, especially after about 1800, were mass-produced from moulds, no after-decoration or glazing was required so that the prime cost was low. No wonder Wedgwood rejoiced '. . . I hope white hands will continue in fashion and then we may continue to make black teapots'.

Today's collectors of these once everyday table and ornamental wares have a good (but alas out of print and expensive) reference-book to resort to. This is Capt. M. H. Grant's *The Makers of Black Basaltes* (W. Blackwood & Sons, 1910). Various other books, especially those on Wedgwood wares, illustrate a range of basalt wares.

191. A rare and large-size marked Wedgwood & Bentley basalt ewer. This was probably an ornamental piece rather than a jug for use, as this partnership related only to ornamental wares. *c.* 1770–80. $11\frac{1}{4}$ inches high.

192. A set of three superb Wedgwood & Bentley basalt vases. This basic shape also occurs in marbled creamware. *c.* 1770–80. $12\frac{3}{4}$ and $8\frac{1}{2}$ inches high.

193. A rare, impressed marked
'Neale & Co', basalt portrait
medallion in the Wedgwood style.
c. 1778–86. 11¼ inches high.

194. A fine set of marked 'Neale &
Co' basalt vases in the Wedgwood
style, showing superb workmanship. c. 1778–86. 9½ and 8½ inches
high.

195. A fine-quality and rare, marked 'H Palmer. Hanley' (in circular form) basalt vase in the Wedgwood style. *c.* 1770–78. 11¾ inches high.

196. A really superbly potted Staffordshire basalt large vase and cover, with deeply under-cut reliefs. Unmarked. *c.* 1770–75. 23¼ inches high.

Opposite page

197. Two of a set of three documentary basalt vases of magnificent design and workmanship. Signed 'Voyez, sculpt 1769', the plinths impressed 'Made by H. Palmer, Hanley, Staffordse'. 15½ and 13½ inches high. For an account of Jean Voyez, see a paper by R. J. Charleston published in the *Transactions of the English Ceramic Circle*, Vol. 5, part 1, 1960.

198. A fine-quality marked Wedgwood & Bentley basalt teapot decorated with encaustic enamelled decoration in a typical manner (see also Plates 153 and 200). *c.* 1770–80. 5¾ inches high.

199. A fine and typical pair of marked 'Wedgwood' basalt vases decorated in the so-called Etruscan manner with encaustic colours. *c.* 1780–90. 12¾ inches high.

200. A fine-quality Wedgwood basalt inkwell and pen-holder, and a cup and saucer, each decorated with typical encaustic colours. *c.* 1780–90. Inkstand $3\frac{1}{2}$ inches high.

201. Two marked 'Wedgwood' basalt vases (as Plate 199 but without covers) decorated in a typical classical-style in encaustic colours. *c.* 1780–90. $8\frac{1}{2}$ inches high.

202. An important, marked
'Wedgwood' basalt vase, decorated
in the classical-style with red and
white encaustic enamels. *c.* 1780–
90. 12 inches high.

203. An elegant and marked 'Wedgwood' basalt vase, decorated in an unusual classical-style with encaustic enamels. *c.* 1780–90. $11\frac{3}{4}$ inches high.

204. A rare, impressed marked
'Spode' basalt vase and cover. All
Spode basalt is rare and is of fine
quality, this vase is particularly
unusual. *c.* 1790. 7½ inches high.

205. An attractive impressed marked 'Spode' basalt creamer with Chinese-style moulded panels. *c.* 1795. 5 inches high.

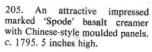

206. A rare, impressed marked 'Spode' basalt teapot, matching the creamer shown above. *c.* 1795. $5\frac{1}{4}$ inches high.

207. An impressed marked 'Neale
& Co' engine-turned basalt teapot,
with metal tip to spout, a not
unusual feature, see Plate 210. *c.*
1780–86. 6 inches high.

208. A fine-quality 'B & W'
marked basalt teapot by Birch &
Whitehead of Shelton. Note the
narrow end to the spout to aid the
addition of a metal-reinforcing col-
lar. *c.* 1796. 4½ inches high.

209. A rare, Caughley basalt teapot, bearing the standard impressed marked 'SALOPIAN' mark. *c.* 1785–95. 5 inches high.

210. A rare, Coalport basalt teapot, bearing the impressed mark 'BRADLEY & CO. COALPORT'. *c.* 1797–1800. 4¼ inches high.

211. An engine-turned basalt creamer, impressed marked 'SHORTHOSE & CO'. *c.* 1817–22. 5¾ inches high.

212. A rare, impressed marked 'P & F W' basalt-covered sugar-bowl. The initial-mark relating to Peter and Francis Warburton of Cobridge. *c.* 1795–1802. 5 inches high.

213. A rare, but damaged (handles missing) marked 'POOLE, LAKIN & CO' basalt vase of fine quality. *c.* 1795. 7¾ inches high.

214. An elegant engine-turned basalt jug, with slightly lustred border-motif. Unmarked. 7¾ inches high.

215. A simply turned basalt-covered sugar-bowl bearing the impressed mark 'HARDING', probably referring to Ralph Harding of Shelton. *c.* 1825. 4 inches high.

216. A marked Leeds basalt waste-bowl of a rare type, bearing the impressed mark 'Hartley Greens & Co. Leeds Pottery'. *c.* 1800–10. Diameter 6½ inches.

217. A rare, basalt copy of a 1741 German medal, bearing the problem impressed mark 'Walkers'. *c.* 1800. Diameter 2¼ inches.

218. A rare, impressed marked Davenport basalt waste-bowl. Although most pottery manufacturers of the 1790–1820 period made some basalt, the marked work of some firms is very rarely found. *c.* 1800–10. Diameter 7 inches.

219. A basalt teapot, bearing the impressed mark 'J Glass, Hanley'. *c.* 1820–30. 11 inches long.

220. A fine-quality basalt teapot, bearing under the handle the impressed initials 'ES'. Many similar pots bear such impressed initials, and as yet it is not proved whether these relate to the manufacturing firm or to an individual workman. *c.* 1815–25. 5¾ inches high.

221. An oval basalt covered sugar-bowl with the impressed mark 'Eastwood', as used by William Baddeley of Eastwood, Hanley, in the 1802–22 period. 5½ inches high.

222. An important Baddeley 'Eastwood'-marked basalt coffee pot, a swan knob replacing the popular Widow knob found with so many basalt pots. *c.* 1815–22. 9¼ inches high.

223. An impressed marked 'Leeds Pottery' basalt creamer. *c.* 1810–20. $5\frac{1}{4}$ inches high.

224. A tasteful, impressed marked 'WEDGWOOD' basalt footed bowl. Wedgwood designs are seldom over-decorated; compare this bowl with the teapot Plate 225. *c.* 1820. $4\frac{1}{4}$ inches high.

225. An unmarked basalt relief-moulded teapot, the side-panels commemorating the victories in Portugal and Spain. Incorporating the date 21 June 1813. *c.* 1815. 10¼ inches long.

Jasper

It is strange that as yet no book has been devoted to this English ceramic body, which in 1774 its 'inventor' Josiah Wedgwood rightly described as a body '... of exquisite beauty and delicacy ... receiving colours through its whole substance, in a manner which no other body ... has been known to do'. An uncommon example is shown in Colour Plate VIII, uncommon in shape and subject but not in the basic technique of applying separately formed white Jasper reliefs onto a coloured ground.

While in 1774 in his early report on the new body, Wedgwood stated that it was coloured 'through its whole substance', in practice it was often found better to tint only the surface. This is known as 'Jasper-dip' and the portrait-plaque shown in Plate 226 is of this type as is evidenced by the chip, top-left, exposing the white underlying body. The vase shown in Colour Plate VIII is also of 'Jasper-dip' as can be seen by the inside at the top, also by the white turned-out groove at the top and bottom of the main body.

On the finest quality Jasper pieces the white relief-motif has been sharpened-up or undercut by hand. The plaque shown in Plate 226 is a case in point, the curls of hair and the ribbon and lower parts of the cloak being undercut after the relief was removed from the separate mould where it was formed and applied to the blue ground. A selection of fine Wedgwood and Bentley period portrait-plaques (c. 1777–80) are seen in Plate 227, and later Wedgwood ones in Plate 229. The long oval ones shown near the top of Plate 229 are of a rare and costly type known as 'three-colour', that is, the ground is of two different coloured Jaspers, the third colour being the white. Other 'three-colour' pieces are shown in Plates 235–36, but rare and desirable as these multi-coloured pieces are, I prefer some of the simple two-colour products, for example the charming little creamer seen in Plate 233, or the vase shown in Plate 239.

It is often very difficult or impossible to date accurately these wares, apart from the later post-1860 pieces which can bear the three-letter dating system (Plate 240 and page 114), so that the original 1803 account and the related teapot shown in Plates 230–31 are of great interest. Also of interest are the many small objects to be found—all too rarely nowadays!— even the scent-bottles (Plates 236 and 238) are relatively common compared with objects such as the egg-cup shown in Plate 237.

As with the basalt-body, or in fact with any other basic type of ceramic ware, one manufacturer was not left to enjoy alone the fruits of his expertise and Wedgwood's Jasper ware had many imitators. The Adams firm, for example, produced such wares from the early 1800s (Plate 241) into the present century (Plate 243). Several other Staffordshire manufacturers produced plainly marked specimens. Many other examples do not bear a maker's mark—they are not less beautiful because of this omission (Plate 242) although many collectors shun such examples, as if the mark was more important than the object!

174

Although some very commercial Jasper wares were produced in the second half of the nineteenth century (Plate 244), the Jasper wares, without any additional decoration, represent one of the most decorative forms of British ceramic.

226. A typical fine-quality, marked 'WEDGWOOD' jasper portrait medallion, showing some undercutting of the reliefs. The chip at the top shows the underlying white jasper below the blue-dipped surface. *c.* 1790. $3\frac{3}{4}$ and 3 inches.

Following page
227. A selection of rare, marked Wedgwood & Bentley blue jasper-ware portrait medallions. *c.* 1777–80. Benjamin Franklin, top right, 4 inches high.

228. An imposing, impressed marked 'WEDGWOOD' black jasper Homeric vase with white reliefs. *c.* 1810. 18¾ inches high.

Following pages
229. A selection of typical Wedgwood jasper-ware medallions, the lower six with a blue ground, the upper ones in the desirable three-colour style, that is, two-colour jasper grounds on which the white reliefs were applied. *c.* 1780–1820. Centre, portrait of George III, 2½ inches high.

230. A Wedgwood account of August 1803, issued from the firm's London, York Street, retail establishment and relating to an American order. The first item—'Deep blue and white Jasper cameo ... upright teapot'—at 14/6d is shown on the right. Other jasper colour combinations listed are yellow and white, lilac and white, also plain light blue, lilac and yellow.

London Augt 29th 1803

J. M. Dyckman Esqr

Bought of Josiah Wedgwood & Byerley

Potters TO HER MAJESTY

And their Royal Highnesses the DUKES of YORK & CLARENCE.

N.B. Their Manufactures both useful and ornamental, fixed at the lowest prices for Ready Money, are sold at their Warehouse in YORK STREET, St. James's Square, and no other place in Town, but goods ordered for the Ports of Bristol, Liverpool & Hull, or for any of the intermediate Towns, or for Scotland or Ireland, will be most advantageously forwarded from their Manufactory at ETRURIA, in Staffordshire.

SMD
New York

— Deep blue and white jasper cameo subjects in Compartments.

	£	s
1 Upright Tea Pot		14
1 Cream Ewer and cover		8
1 Bowl		12
2 Bread & Butter Plates	1	16
1 Tea Caddy		2 6
12 Tea Cups & Saucers	3	12
12 Coffee Cans &c	4	10
1 Sugar		10
1 Flower Pot		18
Box to pack the above		
Deep blue & white cups		
1 Thut Basket		18
1 Do yellow & white		18
2 Do lilac and white	1	16
Deep blue & white jasper		
1 Sweet Meat Basket		6
1 Do light blue		6
1 Do lilac		6
1 Do yellow		6
4 Boxes &c		6
Case with Iron bands		10
	£19	5

231. An impressed marked 'WEDGWOOD' deep-blue and white jasper 'upright' teapot, that listed in the 1803 account and charged originally at 14/6d (Plate 230). Matching tea wares ordered were cream ewer and cover, waste-bowl, sugar-bowl, tea-caddy (a rather surprising item at this period), two bread and butter plates, 12 teacups and saucers and 12 coffee cans (straight sided cups) and saucers.

232. An important, marked 'WEDGWOOD' black-dip jasper-ware pot-pourri vase with pierced cover. *c.* 1820. 24 inches high.

233. A charming and fine-quality marked 'WEDGWOOD' solid blue jasper creamer with white reliefs. *c.* 1810–15. 2½ inches high.

234. An impressed marked 'WEDGWOOD' blue-dipped jasper plaque with applied white relief-motifs. *c.* 1800–20. 12 inches long.

235. Two marked 'WEDGWOOD' coffee cans and saucers and a covered custard cup in the rare and expensive three-colour technique. *c.* 1810–20. Custard cup $2\frac{3}{4}$ inches high.

236. Two rare Wedgwood scent bottles. Flat, oval, and in three colour jasper (green, lilac, and white). Two of several designs made also in different basic shapes, see also Plate 238. *c.* 1800–20. $3\frac{1}{8}$ inches high.

237. Two very rare Wedgwood hollow egg-stands in grey and cane-coloured jasper. *c.* 1800–10. 1½ inches high.

238. Two flat, circular scent bottles in blue jasper, with silver screw-covers and jasper stopper. Representative, with those in Plate 236, of several similar, charming and rare, small items found in jasper. *c.* 1810–20. 2 inches high, without stopper.

239. An imposing impressed marked 'WEDGWOOD' blue and white jasper 'torch' pot-pourri vase with pierced cover and billing dove finial. *c.* 1820–25. 7¼ inches high.

240. A pale blue and white jasper vase and cover with impressed date-letter for 1861, showing that some mid-Victorian Wedgwood can be tasteful and of fine quality. Many 18th-century designs were produced throughout the 19th century—having a timeless appeal. 11¾ inches high.

241. A fine-quality light-blue jasper tankard, bearing the impressed mark 'ADAMS'. *c.* 1810–20. 3¾ inches high.

242. A fine-quality slatey-blue and white pot-pourri vase, of a type found in several colour combinations and sizes, but without a maker's mark. Perhaps Adams or Turner. *c.* 1790. 9 inches high.

243. A selection of early-20th-century blue and white Adams jasperwares. Some examples bear impressed marks such as 'ADAMS. ESTB.D. 1657. TUNSTALL. ENGLAND', arranged in four lines.
Pottery Gazette 1906.

Opposite page
244. A page from a wholesaler's catalogue of the 1880s showing typical non-Wedgwood jasperwares of the period. These objects do not normally bear a manufacturer's mark, but they are of Staffordshire origin, perhaps by James Dudson of Hanley.

Overleaf
245. A page from a 20th-century Wedgwood catalogue showing typical dark blue and white jasperwares of the 1900–10 period although some shapes—such as the tea wares in the top row—have been made over a very long period. These later wares will probably have three impressed letters—the last signifying the year (see page 114) together with the word 'ENGLAND'. Later examples will be marked 'MADE IN ENGLAND'.

4744

4745

4746

4747

4748

4749

4750

4751

4752

4754

4757

4753

4755

4756

4758

4759

4760

4761

4762

"WEDGWOOD" BAS-RELIEF WARE.

Sugar box 146 Shape.

Teapot. 146 Shape.

Cream 146 Shape.

Coffee pot 129.

Teacup & Saucer.

Jug Upright Shape E.P. Propellor Mount.

Sugar box S.t Louis Shape.

Teapot S.t Louis Shape.

Cream S.t Louis Shape.

Jug Dutch Shape.

Teapot Brewster Shape.

Teapot Stand Shape. B

Orange Shape Jug.

Upright Mug.

Open Sugar 3"

Dutch Jug 2½"

Etruscan Jug.

Coffee cup & Saucer.

Chocolate Jug.

Upright Loving Mug.

JOSIAH WEDGWOOD & SONS L.TD ETRURIA, STOKE ON TRENT.

Turner's Body

The aim of this section is not to discuss the varied wares made by John Turner (1738–87) and by his sons at Lane End, for this object has been admirably accomplished by Bevis Hillier in his book *The Turners of Lane End: Master Potters of the Industrial Revolution* (Cory, Adams & Mackay, London, 1965), but rather to illustrate typical examples of a special whitish refined semi-porcelain body which I term 'Turner's body'. These relief-decorated wares were not, however, confined to the Turners, but were copied by many of the leading English potters of the 1785–1825 period.

Simeon Shaw in his *History of the Staffordshire Potteries* (privately printed in Hanley in 1829) wrote: 'About 1780, he (John Turner) discovered a vein of fine clay on the land at Green Dock . . . From this he obtained all his supplies for manufacturing his beautiful and excellent *Stone Ware Pottery*, of a cane-colour; which he formed into very beautiful jugs with ornamental designs, and the most tasteful articles of domestic use'. Samples of Turner's 'tasteful articles of domestic use' are shown in Plates 246–50.

The workmanship of these jugs and mugs is superb and I tend to prefer these uncoloured relief-decorated wares to the similar but two-coloured Jasper wares discussed in the previous section. It will be observed that several of these objects have silver or silver-plated rims or covers, and an advertisement issued by Turner's London retail establishment particularly mentions 'mugs and jugs with silver rims and covers' (see my *Illustrated Encyclopaedia of British Pottery and Porcelain*, Herbert Jenkins, London, 1964, p. 325). These silver embellishments can enable the pot to be dated by reference to the date of hall-marking (Plate 251). John and William Turner continued production from the period of their father's death in 1787 until at least 1804 when John retired. In July 1806 the brothers were declared bankrupt, but William Turner appears to have continued potting for many years, until 1829 when a sale of his stock of Earthenware, Potters' utensils and the like was advertised. This stock included '. . . black teapots and cream ewers; ditto stone and ornaments, beautifully figured &c . . . .' These figured 'stone' wares could well be the later products in Turner's body.

Without the advantage of an impressed name-mark it is almost impossible to distinguish between the wares of Turner and those of his Staffordshire contemporaries making this ware. Certainly the marked 'Adams' examples shown in Plates 251–53 rival in quality the best of Turners.

Closely allied to the Turner wares we have the rather deeper coloured cane-wares with a slightly more porous surface-texture (the Turner body has a very slight and pleasing gloss). A good Mayer example is illustrated in Plate 254 and a Wedgwood teapot in Plate 255. Contrasting with these matt cane-wares we have a class of slightly glazed Turner-type wares, sometimes with the use of contrasting coloured reliefs in the Jasper manner. The Herculaneum factory at Liverpool made some excellent essays in this style (Plates 256–57).

The so-called Yorkshire 'Castleford' wares are closely related to the relief-decorated

British Pottery

Turner wares. The body is a refined, white semi-translucent stoneware, in appearance very similar to the Victorian Parian body. Tea wares, especially teapots with hinged, or sliding covers, were much favoured, and a blue-enamel edging is characteristic of the whole class (Plates 260–63). The term 'Castleford' should be regarded only as referring to the general type, and in fact most examples were probably not made at this Yorkshire pottery.

Lastly in this section we can very briefly mention the darker Turner-type stonewares so popular early in the Victorian era for the production of relief-moulded jugs and other wares. Some typical examples from the William Ridgway factory are shown in Plates 264–65. These are vastly different in style from the early Turner jugs of the 1780s, yet the basic similarity of unpainted relief-patterned refined stoneware is displayed.

246. A fine-quality impressed marked 'TURNER' porcelainous stoneware tankard with plated rim. *c.* 1786–1800. 6¼ inches high.

247. An impressed marked 'TUR-
NER', porcelainous-stoneware jug
with hunting subject reliefs and
silver rim and cover with year-letter
for 1799, 8¾ inches high.

248. Another fine, marked 'TUR-
NER' hunting jug of a popular
type. The plated rim by Thomas
Law & Co. of Sheffield. *c.* 1795–
1805. 8¼ inches high.

249. A marked 'TURNER' porcelainous-stoneware tankard, with
engine-turned border at the foot.
Plated rim. *c.* 1800–1805. 6¼
inches high.

250. A handsome, impressed
marked 'TURNER' jug with figure
reliefs. The border- and side-reliefs
as Plate 247. *c.* 1795–1800. 10¾
inches high.

252. An imposing, marked 'ADAMS', porcelainous-stoneware jug with crisply moulded figure reliefs. *c.* 1800–10. 10 inches high, without plated cover.

Opposite page
251. A superb, impressed marked 'ADAMS' porcelainous-stoneware jug in the Turner style with classical-type figure reliefs. Silver rim by Thomas Law & Co. of Sheffield with year-letter for 1807. 8½ inches high.

253. A rare, marked 'ADAMS', porcelainous-stoneware jug in the Turner style, the reliefs depicting a contemporary scene. *c.* 1795–1805. 9 inches high.

254. A finely potted cane-ware waste-bowl, bearing the impressed mark 'E. MAYER'. This talented Hanley potter worked from the 1780s to 1804. 3½ inches high.

255. A fine-quality Wedgwood caneware teapot and cover and a matching bowl, upturned to show early upper- and lower-case 'Wedgwood' mark. *c.* 1790–8. 4½ inches high.

256. A rare, impressed marked 'HERCULANEUM' (Liverpool) porcelainous-stoneware covered (tobacco?) box, with green-coloured reliefs and brown inlaid borders. *c.* 1800–1810. 8 inches high.

257. A magnificent, impressed marked 'HERCULANEUM' (Liverpool) porcelainous-stoneware teapot and cover, the body dipped, or washed, with a deep reddish-brown stain, upon which are applied the charming and crisp reliefs. *c.* 1810–15. 10¾ inches long.

258. A rare Castleford-type porcelainous-stoneware jug commemorating a naval victory. *c.*
1810. 5 inches high.

259. A simple relief-moulded and
enamelled Castleford-type porcelainous-stoneware presentation
jug, inscribed 'J. M. Manchester,
1796'. 6¾ inches high.

260. A rare relief-moulded Castleford-type teapot and covered sugar-bowl with hand-painted scenic panels. *c.* 1815. Teapot 5½ inches high.

261. An unmarked Castleford-type moulded porcelainous-stoneware covered sugar-bowl with typical blue-enamel lining. *c.* 1810–20. 5½ inches high.

262. A rare and superb unmarked Castleford-type teapot, the central panel coloured with a deep-chocolate ground to throw up the relief in the Wedgwood manner. *c.* 1810–20. 5½ inches high.

263. A fine-quality relief-moulded Castleford-type teapot. The description is a generic one, and pots of this type were made at several unidentified factories. The impressed number '22' is often found under the base. *c.* 1810–20. 6¾ inches high.

264. Representative pieces from a relief-moulded dessert service in a putty-coloured stoneware, shown with the relevant page from the William Ridgway pattern-book, *c.* 1835–40.

265. Three typical, early Victorian relief-moulded stoneware jugs of differing colours. Bearing the helpful mark 'Published by W Ridgway Son & Co Hanley. September 1st, 1840'. Centre example 9¾ inches high.

Ironstone-type Bodies

Various attempts had been made early in the nineteenth century to perfect a new and inexpensive, yet durable, earthenware body. By far the most successful was 'Mason's Patent Ironstone China', a much publicised trade-name and one used as an impressed mark on many pieces. The name 'Ironstone China' quickly caught the public's fancy implying as it did a tough yet delicate china-like ware.

The patent was entered in July 1813 under the name of Charles James Mason of Fenton in the Staffordshire Potteries. The resulting heavy durable body was extensively employed for dinner and dessert services and was gaily, if freely, painted with colourful 'Japan' or other Oriental-inspired designs. The potting and general standard of decoration was not superb, but the novel new colourful ware was able to compete most favourably with the most costly porcelains of the period and a huge market was quickly established. Typical examples are shown in Plates 266–76. The standard printed Mason mark is reproduced below. This was used by Mason's firm from about 1815 and by his successors for the greater part of the nineteenth century. The name is still perpetuated today by Messrs Mason's Ironstone China Ltd. (see page 424.)

So successful was Mason's Patent Ironstone China that practically every potter of the 1830–80 period made versions of it, under various names such as—'Granite China', 'Opaque China', 'Stone China', 'Stone ware', and many others. Such wares proved highly saleable especially in the export markets, suffering little if any damage in transit and standing up well to hard wear. It was a robust ware suited well to the expanding world-markets of the nineteenth century. At its best Ironstone closely rivals porcelain, but for everyday use it has many advantages and today's so-called 'hotel wares' are closely related to the Victorian Ironstone china.

The full story of Mason's and of the rival Ironstone-type wares is told in my *Illustrated Guide to Mason's Patent Ironstone China* (Barrie & Jenkins, London, 1971).

266. A typical, early Mason's Patent Ironstone dessert service plate, decorated in the colourful but relatively inexpensive 'Japan pattern' in underglaze-blue, with overglaze red, green, and gold. Many such designs were made. Circular impressed mark. *c.* 1813–20. Diameter 8 inches.

Following page
268. A small Chinese-shaped sauce-tureen from a dinner service, decorated with a characteristic so-called 'Japan pattern' in blue, red, green, and gold. Impressed mark. *c.* 1815–25. 7½ inches long.

267. Representative parts of a large Mason's Patent Ironstone dinner service, bearing the impressed mark. The shapes are copied from standard 18th-century Chinese export-market porcelains. *c.* 1815–25. Tureen 13½ inches long.

269. An impressed-marked 'Mason's Patent Ironstone China' centrepiece from a typical dessert service and a matching plate. This shows one of the standard Mason 'Japan patterns'. *c.* 1815–25. Comport 5½ inches high.

270. A handsome, Oriental-styled Mason's Ironstone punch-bowl, bearing the standard printed mark. *c.* 1825–30. Diameter 10¼ inches.

271. A Mason's Ironstone punch-bowl, rather coarsely painted with a Chinese-style formal, floral pattern. Printed mark. *c.* 1830–40. Diameter 11 inches.

Previous pages

272. Part of a fine-quality early Mason's Patent Ironstone dinner service, showing typical shapes. The sauce-boat—one of a pair—is very rare. This and other service patterns occur also on other wares, see Plate 270. *c.* 1813–20. Tureen 13½ inches long.

273. A colourful Mason's Patent Ironstone dessert service. The Chinese-styled 'Mogul' pattern has a printed outline which was later coloured-over by hand, a standard practice. The shapes are rather rare. Printed mark. *c.* 1820–30. Centrepiece 12½ inches long.

274. A rather broadly painted, impressed marked Mason's Ironstone tureen, cover and stand of characteristic shape from a dessert service of the 1815–25 period. 7 inches high.

275. A colourful, impressed marked 'Mason's Patent Ironstone China' dessert service tureen, cover, and stand, showing a characteristic form of the 1815–20 period. 7¼ inches high.

276. A massive Mason's Ironstone vase (cover missing), decorated in a typical mock-Oriental manner. Blue base and red ground to the main part. *c.* 1840–50. 22¾ inches high.

277. An Ashworth re-issue of a standard Mason tureen-shape and printed pattern, together with a plate from the same service. Printed Mason's mark, but impressed potting-marks 7·06 for July 1906. Tureen 11¼ inches high.

Opposite page
278. Some typical miniature or 'toy' vases in Mason's Patent Ironstone showing some characteristic shapes and patterns. *c.* 1815–30. Centre vase 8 inches high.

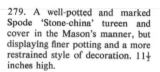

279. A well-potted and marked Spode 'Stone-china' tureen and cover in the Mason's manner, but displaying finer potting and a more restrained style of decoration. 11½ inches high.

280. A blue-printed 'Stone-china' tureen from a long dinner service, bearing the initial mark of John & William Ridgway—one of the leading makers of services in this durable body. *c.* 1820–30. Tureen 6 inches high.

Lustre Decoration

Lustre decoration is formed by applying thin metallic films to ceramics. On pottery t main effects are silver-lustre or copper-lustre. These can be applied in two basic ways: embellishments to an enamelled object, or as a complete or near complete covering to gi the effect, partially at least, of a silver or copper object.

Various claims were made in the early nineteenth century by persons supposed to ha introduced lustre, and the question is still not settled. It can be stated, however, that lustre-effects on British pottery are of nineteenth-, not eighteenth-century date and process is still used today. At first silver-lustre (derived from platinum) was used purely a secondary embellishment, either a silver-lustre rim was applied or special details we picked out in lustre. The jug (Plate 281) of c. 1810 is a good example of this practice. Oth wares, mainly jugs, were decorated in silver-lustre by the 'resist' process, where parts of object to be left white were temporarily resisted with wax or a paper cut-out so that lustre solution applied to the whole would not effect the resisted portions. A similar eff was achieved by stencilling. Plate 283 shows a simple resist-type silver-lustre jug, while rare, marked 'Rogers' dish displays the same effect achieved perhaps by scratching lustre film away before firing.

Other silver- or pink-lustre designs comprise hand-painted landscapes including prom ently placed buildings. Typical examples are here shown in Colour Plate IX and in Pla 284, 286. This style is not confined to the Staffordshire Potteries nor to earthenwares. T pleasing graduations of tone were achieved by first using a thin, weak wash and ov painting this where a darker tone was required. The dated 1815 jug shown in Plate 286 i good example of this type.

A pleasing variation of silver-lustre is called 'splash-lustre' or sometimes 'Sunderla lustre' in the belief that the effect is confined to the Sunderland potteries. This is not so. T circular ink-well shown in Plate 287 has incised into the base the inscription 'Thos. Mass Burslem. 1820' and the Wedgwood firm made similar splash-lustre as did various otl manufacturers who did not mark their products.

The Sunderland potters did indeed make a vast quantity of lustre-ware and examples shown in Plates 288–90. Many of these specimens combine printed patterns with fre painted lustre borders, and such pieces could be very cheaply decorated by inexpens labour. A series of hanging-plaques (Plates 288, 290) commanded a great sale and decorative and often amusing.

A series of wares totally covered in silver-lustre, originally intended to emulate sil objects, was made in the 1840-70 period, some being shown at the 1851 Exhibition.

It will be observed that the silver- or platinum-lustre was applied to a white body, but slightly later copper-lustre (derived from gold) was normally applied to a dark cl coloured body, although to give certain contrasting decorative effects white bands w applied over the darker body and the inside of a jug or similar article would be washed w

214

a white slip to give a better, more expensive looking, finish. Two dated examples are shown in Plates 291–92. For a lengthy period from about 1840 a good range of inexpensive copper-lustre earthenware was produced, often with simple, rather cottagy, enamelling over the lustre. Such wares were made by the smaller firms and very rarely bear a maker's mark.

Copper-lustre in particular has great charm and looks very well with oak furniture. Its appeal has not been forgotten by later firms, and reproductions have been made in the present century. Lustre-decorated pottery is confined to the British potters. Except for rare documentary specimens, it is still reasonably priced and affords an interesting and decorative field for the collector.

281. An attractive relief-moulded Staffordshire earthenware jug with hunting-subject. The edge and border picked-out in 'silver' (platinum) lustre. *c.* 1810–15. 8¼ inches high.

282. A silver-lustre Staffordshire earthenware dish bearing the impressed mark 'ROGERS'. Some of the contrasting white, resisted design, particularly the tendrils, appears to be scratched. *c.* 1815–25. 17 inches long.

283. A typical, so-called resist-lustre jug. The main design is a blue print, over which a wax-resist was painted before the silver-lustre was applied to the exposed ground. *c.* 1815–25. 4¾ inches high.

284. A relief-moulded Sunderland earthenware plate, the centre painted in pink lustre with a version of the popular 'house' pattern. Impressed mark 'DIXON AUSTIN & CO'. *c.* 1820–30. Diameter 7½ inches.

285. A silver-lustre resist jug of a standard shape, but bearing the very rare impressed mark 'BOARDMAN', perhaps relating to a Liverpool manufacturer. Jugs of this type are very seldom marked. *c.* 1820. 4¼ inches high.

Opposite page

286. A noble and well-potted pink-lustre 'house' pattern presentation-jug, inscribed 'Richard & Eliz[th] Wooten, Sutton Cheney, Leicestershire 1815'. Jugs were a popular gift, and the dated examples form helpful landmarks. 6½ inches high.

Above

287. A documentary Staffordshire splash-lustre inkwell, incised in the base 'Thos. Massey, Burslem, 1820'. 2¾ inches high.

288. A rare, marked 'Albion Pottery' (Newcastle-on-Tyne) splash-lustre and printed wall-plaque. Similar plaques were made at many northern potteries and have great charm. See also Plate 290. *c.* 1850. 9½ and 8½ inches.

289. A typical Sunderland lustre mug, the print showing the famous local bridge opened in 1796. Most jugs and other Sunderland wares depicting this bridge were made after 1830. Printed signed 'Scott & Sons, Southwick'. *c.* 1830–38. 5¼ inches high.

290. A typical Sunderland lustred wall-plaque with copper-lustre and pink splash-lustre border with unusual 'message'. Impressed marked 'DAWSON'. *c.* 1840–50. 9¾ × 8¾ inches.

291. A simple Staffordshire, earthenware, copper-lustre mug bearing the relatively early date 1826, on a yellow band. 3 inches high.

292. An interesting copper-lustre jug with pink-lustre 'house' design in the central band and inscribed 'To the R^t Honourable Lord Bagot, 1832. This jug was made from clay from the Yeatsall Brickyard'. 5½ inches high.

Mocha Decoration

A range of basically inexpensive utilitarian earthenwares such as beer-mugs and jugs we[re]
made with a tree-like design, known as 'Mocha'.

The earliest recorded dated example is the 1799 mug shown in Plate 293 but Mocha [is]
basically a nineteenth-century style of decoration and was achieved by a simple chemic[al]
reaction. A colourant of an acid nature was applied as a blob or simple line to an alkali[ne]
ground-colour which had been specially applied in an added band. The acid colourant-[
called 'tea'—reacted with the ground to form rapidly a tree-like growth. This growth cou[ld]
be arranged to some extent by inclining the object to arrange the flow or growth.

While, in general, such Mocha wares were unmarked and made by smaller firms or larg[e]
non-Staffordshire potteries, some rare examples were made by Spode. One of the fe[w]
contemporary descriptions of this mode of decoration was written by Charles Dicke[ns]
when writing of a visit to the Spode Works at Stoke-on-Trent in 1852, although at th[at]
period the factory was under the control of W. T. Copeland.

Like many inexpensive utilitarian earthenwares, the Mocha pieces have an appeali[ng]
simple charm.

293. The earliest recorded dated mocha-decorated mug, showing typical tree-like motifs and the base. 3 inches high.

294. A rare, impressed marked 'SPODE' cream-ground spill-vase with moulded border and mocha decoration, a style normally confined to inexpensive utilitarian objects. *c.* 1820–30. 5 inches high.

295. A typical kitchen-jug with inexpensive banded and mocha decoration. Marked 'T. G. GREEN & CO. LTD.' (of Church Gresley, Burton-on-Trent), one of the leading manufacturers of this class of ware. *c.* 1890–1900. 6½ inches high.

William Ridgway Earthenware

The companion to this book, *British Porcelain: An Illustrated Guide*, includes a section on the fine, but little understood, Ridgway porcelain. This brief double-page spread illustrates some of the equally little-known pottery, as made by William Ridgway after the John & William Ridgway partnership had been terminated in November 1830.

Although William Ridgway was not, like his brother John, to aspire to become Potter to Queen Victoria, he was to own six factories at Hanley and Shelton. These produced in the main useful earthenwares. The wares here shown are of fine quality, made of a delicately tinted bluish-mauve body. These typical William Ridgway wares of the 1830–45 period do not bear a mark—only a painted pattern-number—consequently the wares of this class are often attributed to other works; in fact, the floral encrusted cup and saucer was sold to me as Rockingham!

Luckily, we have the original Ridgway pattern book, in which these and many other similar objects are drawn, and this enables some, at least, of the William Ridgway earthenwares to be identified. Our meagre understanding of so much nineteenth-century unmarked pottery is due mainly to the fact that so few of the factory-records have been preserved. Many pages from the Ridgway pattern-book, together with matching objects are shown in my *Illustrated Guide to Ridgway Porcelains* (Barrie & Jenkins, London, 1972).

296. A rare, floral-encrusted William Ridgway cabinet cup and saucer in the characteristic bluish-mauve earthenware. Pattern-number 224. Diameter of saucer $5\frac{1}{4}$ inches.

297. A typical William Ridgway floral-patterned bluish-mauve earthenware jug of the 1835–40 period. Pattern-number 56. $7\frac{1}{4}$ inches high.

298. A William Ridgway bluish-mauve earthenware candlestick—one of a pair, showing the popular cornucopia floral design. *c.* 1835–40. 8 inches high.

Printing

Printing as a form of ceramic decoration dates back to the middle of the eighteenth century—mainly on porcelain and enamels but sometimes on pottery articles such as tiles. Here we are mainly concerned with nineteenth-century printed earthenwares.

As a form of mass-production printing may appear to be a complicated process, but once the copper-plates had been engraved (or purchased ready-engraved) the potter could decorate in a competent manner a vast array of wares using only semi-skilled labour and certainly without the expense of employing trained artists.

The basic methods of production can usefully be explained here. The key to the whole operation is the engraver, whose task it is first to design a suitable pattern or to adapt to the shapes of the articles a published design—perhaps a printed view. This motif is then transferred to a flat sheet (later a roller) of copper by means of cut or etched lines or dots, Plate 300. The deeper or thicker the line, or dot, or the closer these are together, the deeper will be the colour. Once this laborious task is completed—one copper-plate for each size or shape of article—then the copper-plate is ready to be used. Thick oily ceramic pigment, normally cobalt blue, is rubbed into the recessed design, the surface of the copper-plate is then rubbed clean and special tissue-like transfer paper is applied to the heated and charged copper-plate, and both are placed under pressure.

The pigment is thus transferred to the paper, which is then lifted from the copper-plate and passed to a female helper who cuts away the surplus paper. A printress then very carefully positions the cut-charged paper onto an unglazed plate or other object (Plate 299). The paper is subsequently soaked off and normally the object is then lightly fired to burn out the oil in the pigment. Then the object is glazed so that the blue design becomes an underglaze print. The factory-mark, often incorporating the name of that one pattern, is engraved on the same copper-plate as the main design (Plate 319). Once transferred to the paper the mark is cut off and applied to the back—hence a mark is often particular to that one, mass-produced, design and will be printed in the same colour.

Having explained the basic essentials of the printing technique it will be obvious that it was only employed when fairly long runs of a particular design were required—or thought to be required! One would not go to the expense of engraving a copper-plate for a single object or even for a run of twenty or so; much less would one engrave a costly set of coppers for a service, if only a few were to be made. Of course, with the passage of time the majority of specimens, especially of table wares, will have been broken or otherwise lost to the collector, but no printed design was originally unique.

I have just described underglaze printing but some prints were applied overglaze, that is to a ready-glazed object. Early examples include the salt-glazed plates (Plates 102–3) and the early Wedgwood and other creamwares printed by Messrs Sadler & Green of Liverpool. This firm, or rather John Sadler at first, specialised in the printing of tiles (see Plate 505 in the *Illustrated Encyclopaedia of British Pottery and Porcelain*, Herbert Jenkins, London,

228

1966). Wedgwoods sent vast amounts of their creamware to Liverpool to be printed (see Plates 182–83, 301) because before about 1780 the technique was not practiced in the Staffordshire Potteries (a very good article on Sadler & Green the Liverpool printers, by E. N. Stretton is contained in *Collectors Guide*, January 1973). Soon, however, specialist local engravers and printers catered for the growing demand for their talents in the Staffordshire Potteries. These independent printers normally applied their designs over the glaze on ready-prepared blanks and often by way of advertisement their name was incorporated in the design (see Plates 20 and 46 of the above-mentioned *Encyclopaedia*). Later when the various potters carried out their own printing the prints themselves are unsigned.

It was fortunate that the easiest colour to print with under the glaze is cobalt blue and that the popularity for this underglaze-blue pigment had been originally built up by the imported Chinese porcelains—the vast majority of which (and the cheapest) was painted solely in blue. The tin-glazed earthenware (delft) potters first emulated these Oriental porcelains, then from the late 1740s the various English porcelain manufacturers were inspired by Chinese designs. From about the 1780s the potters sought to copy in their cheaper earthenware Chinese porcelains also the English porcelain designs, with the help of underglaze-blue prints.

The fine dinner-plate (Plate 302) bearing the impressed initial-mark of Joshua Heath of Hanley bears a blue-printed copy of a Chinese original and is also very close to a Caughley porcelain design of the 1780s. The marked 'Leeds Pottery' mug shown in Plate 303 bears a copy of Hancock's famous print found applied to Worcester porcelain and copied at the Caughley factory. This example underlines the point that much blue-printed pottery was made by non-Staffordshire manufacturers and that the earthenware potters copied in pottery popular porcelain designs. The fine plate shown in Plate 304 bears a reversed copy of the 'Fisherman' design found on Caughley, Liverpool, and Worcester porcelain, although in this case the print is applied to a moulded-edged plate—a form of edging very popular with all earthenware potters, but not with porcelain manufacturers.

The plate shown in Plate 305 bears in printed form a design found on a large quantity of Chinese Export Market porcelain from about 1785 onwards into the nineteenth century. The Chinese-design print on the teapot shown in Plate 306 is of interest as this piece bears the quite early date 1789. The impressed marked 'Turner' centrepiece (Plate 307) bears a further popular Chinese-inspired blue-print, while the supper (or sandwich) set shows a Chinese-styled design applied to a very European object. This supper set is probably the most complex to have been made, the centre covered vase holds a set of egg-cups and the mahogany tray has a diameter of over twenty-seven inches.

In the early part of the nineteenth century the potters, in part at least, forgot their obsession with copying Chinese designs and porcelain patterns. Completely new designs came into fashion and the prints themselves became more accomplished owing to the engravers' use of dots rather than lines. Study for example the platter and tureen shown as Plate 310 and Colour Plate X. Wide borders, normally floral, came into fashion, and various markets started to be especially catered for by the engraving of series of foreign views or the arms of various American States, etc. By this period the Staffordshire potters were supplying the world with decorative and useful wares that they were able to mass-produce at remarkably low cost.

While I do not intend in this brief summary to list the hundreds of manufacturers of blue-printed pottery, it must be stated that the quality was variable—according to the resources of the potter and the pocket of his customers. The leading firms produced superbly potted and finely engraved designs and I will content myself with drawing attention to the marked Spode tureen and stand illustrated in Plate 311—one of this firm's standard designs—but what a show such a Spode dinner service makes on a dining-table!

The fact that I have progressed into the nineteenth century without mention of the famous Willow pattern may surprise many. Yet I contend that the Willow pattern as we know it today—with figures crossing a bridge under a willow-like tree, with doves flying above, as is shown in Plate 315, is purely a nineteenth-century design. Contrary to popular belief it does not occur on eighteenth-century Caughley porcelain, and it does not seem possible that it was introduced by Thomas Minton while he was apprenticed at this Shropshire factory. The several eighteenth-century Chinese-style landscape designs, as Plates 302, 306–8, do not match the popular Willow pattern. I would also note that I do not support the oft-repeated statement that Thomas Turner of Caughley produced the first blue-printed earthenware. I do not know of any evidence that he made printed pottery!

Between pages 233 and 246 examples of blue-printed pottery from many different potteries, several situated outside the county of Staffordshire, are illustrated. We must remember that in admiring these objects and their printed patterns we are admiring not so much the potter's craft but rather the engraver's art.

In this connection it must be remembered that only the largest firms employed their own skilled engravers and that the host of smaller firms purchased sets of engraved copper-plates from specialist engravers to the trade. Firms such as Bentley Wear & Bourne produced in the 1810–20 period superbly engraved designs, which were purchased by potters up and down the country. In many cases similar 'stock' designs were supplied by the engravers to several different potters, each order differing only in the manufacturer's own trade-mark device. It is a matter of regret that so few engraved designs are signed by the artist-engraver, but this is typical of the time.

While underglaze-blue printing has remained the stable means of inexpensive pottery decoration we can conveniently mention here some almost fair-ground pieces, often charming and interesting, made from the 1840s onwards. These were inexpensive objects such as children's plates or mugs, often decorated with educational or moralistic designs. These objects bear a simply engraved outline-design which was subsequently coloured-in by semi-skilled apprentice labour. The Middlesborough Pottery Company, for example, produced in the 1849–50 period a series of small plates bearing prints depicting 'The Effects of the Bottle' (Plates 327, 329). Messrs Bailey & Ball of Longton produced between 1847 and 1850 an amusing array of printed designs on a registered moulded-edged plate (Plates 328–29). Many other potters made 'A.B.C.' plates, the letters of the alphabet being relief-moulded around the plate rim. Of the same general type we have railway prints and sporting subjects (Plate 329). Pottery of this nature was mass-produced at low cost by the smaller pottery firms. The pieces met a ready demand; they have a primitive charm and are typical of their period.

Helpful reference-books on nineteenth-century British printed pottery include:

Anglo-American China, parts I and II, by Sam Laidacker. (Published by the author at Bristol, Pennsylvania, 2nd edition 1954.) Part I deals with American views, part II with British subjects.

Staffordshire Blue by W. L. Little (Batsford, London, 1969).

Blue and White Transfer Ware by A. W. Coysh (David & Charles, Newton Abbot, 1970).

The Blue-China Book by A. W. Camehl (Dover Publications, New York. The new edition was published in 1971.)

Chapter I of Hugh Wakefield's *Victorian Pottery* (Herbert Jenkins, London, 1962) is also helpful, as is J. K. des Fontaines' paper, 'Underglaze Blue-printed Earthenware with Particular Reference to Spode', contained in the *Transactions of the English Ceramic Circle*, vol. 7, part 2, 1969. Many marks found on printed earthenware can be identified and dated by reference to my *Encyclopaedia of British Pottery and Porcelain Marks* (Herbert Jenkins, London, 1964).

The wares of some individual makers are dealt with in specialist books. For example Spode printed wares are discussed and illustrated in *Spode and his Successors*, A. Hayden (Cassell, London, 1925); *Antique Blue and White Spode*, S. B. Williams (Batsford, London, 1943), and *Spode*, L. Whiter (Barrie & Jenkins, London, 1970).

299. A Wedgwood printress, Miss Sally Shephard, applying the cut transfer-paper with the inked design to the border of an unglazed plate. Rolls of uncut transfers are seen in the background.

300. A Wedgwood engraver, Fred Farmer, at work engraving a flat copper-plate, a pull from which is seen at the back. The responsibility for a successful printed design rests squarely on the engraver's shoulders.

301. A fine, large impressed marked 'WEDGWOOD' cream-ware platter, bearing overglaze printed 'Liverpool birds', design added by Sadler of Liverpool. See also Plate 182. *c.* 1775. $18\frac{1}{2} \times 13\frac{3}{4}$ inches.

302. Two blue-printed Staffordshire pearl-ware dinner plates, part of a set in the fashionable Chinese-type, from which the Willow pattern was later adopted. One plate reversed to show the impressed I H initial-mark as used by John Heath of Hanley. *c.* 1790–1800. Diameter $9\frac{1}{2}$ inches.

303. A marked 'Leeds Pottery' pearl-ware mug bearing an under-glaze-blue-printed copy of a well-known Worcester porcelain design. Many potters copied in earthenware the more expensive porcelain patterns, see also Plate 304. *c.* 1790–1800. 4¾ inches high.

304. An attractive earthenware copy of a well-known porcelain design—the Fisherman pattern found on Caughley, Liverpool, and Worcester porcelains. The moulded edge is, however, a typical feature of creamware and pearl-ware dinner services. *c.* 1790–1800. Diameter 9¾ inches.

305. An impressed marked 'G HARRISON' pearl-ware plate, bearing an underglaze-blue-printed adaptation of a Chinese export-market porcelain design. *c.* 1800–1804. Diameter 9½ inches.

306. A rare, inscribed and dated blue-printed pearl-ware teapot, in the style of the popular Chinese export-market wares and of Worcester, Caughley, and Liverpool porcelains. Inscribed 'S Tonill. 1789'. 5½ inches high.

235

307. An impressed marked 'TUR-
NER' pearl-ware centre-dish from
a dessert service. Printed in
underglaze-blue with a version of
the Elephant pattern, within a
Chinese-style border. *c.* 1785–95.
$14\frac{1}{4}$ inches long.

308. A magnificent and early
Willow-pattern-type supper or
breakfast service in its original
mahogany tray. The central
covered vase contains a pierced
stand for eggs. All complete sets
are rarè, and most comprise only
four-segment dishes around the
central covered dish. Note the
Willow pattern has not yet
acquired the flying doves. *c.* 1810–
15. Diameter $27\frac{1}{2}$ inches.

309. An impressed marked 'ROGERS' blue-printed pearl-ware basket and stand, of which a pair were included with dessert services of the 1800–1820 period. John and George Rogers of Longport, Staffordshire were among the leading manufacturers of blue-printed earthenwares from *c.* 1784 until 1814, and the mark was continued by John Rogers & Son until 1836. 9¼ inches long.

310. A magnificent, large blue-printed platter from a large dinner service. See also Colour Plate X. This print depicts the engagement between the *Chesapeake* and *Shannon*, in which the British vessel was taken by the American. *c.* 1815–20. 21 × 14¼ inches.

Opposite page
311. A well-potted impressed marked 'SPODE' tureen, cover, and stand, decorated with a typical finely engraved underglaze-blue-printed design. Part of a large dinner service of the early 1820s. Stand 17 inches long.

312. A rare Mason's blue-printed pearl-ware (not Ironstone) tureen and ladle, from a large dinner service of the 1810–15 period. Marked 'Semi China. Warranted' in curved form, some few pieces also with 'Masons'. 14 inches long.

313. A large platter from a marked John and William Ridgway 'Stone China' dinner service. The engraving of the underglaze-blue 'India Temple' design is of typically fine quality. *c.* 1815. 21 × 18 inches.

314. A finely engraved blue-printed and impressed marked 'Dillwyn & Co. Swansea' earthenware plate, illustrating the point that good-quality inexpensive blue and white earthenwares were made at several non-Staffordshire factories. *c.* 1811–17. Diameter 9 inches.

315. A typical blue-printed Willow-pattern platter from a large service. This true Willow pattern is purely a post-1800 British design and was made at most 19th-century potteries. This Newcastle-on-Tyne example bears the impressed mark 'PATTERSON & CO. TYNE POTTERY'. *c.* 1850. $12\frac{1}{2} \times 10$ inches.

316. A brown-printed Stafford-shire earthenware plate, depicting 'The Capitol, Washington' and bearing the Royal Arms mark of T. Godwin of Burslem. *c.* 1834–54. Diameter 10½ inches.

317. An unmarked but interesting blue-printed earthenware dish showing a balloon ascent over a crescent. *c.* 1840–45. 12¼ and 9¾ inches.

318. A small, blue-printed, marked 'DAVENPORT' teapot with a matching saucer. A rather cheap, crude engraving but possessing charm. *c.* 1833–40. Pot 4¾ inches high.

319. A 'pull' from an F. & R. Pratt copper-plate showing their 'Asiatic Marine' design, also the way that the factory-mark was incorporated in the relevant copper-plate. This portion of the inked transfer-paper would be cut away and applied to the reverse.

320. A rare, blue-printed Scottish pottery jug bearing the printed mark 'WATSON & CO' of Prestonpans. *c.* 1820–25. 7½ inches high.

321. A finely engraved blue-printed dinner-service plate bearing the impressed mark 'ROGERS' (see also Plate 309). With typical fanciful Chinese-style landscape design. *c.* 1825–36. Diameter 9⅞ inches.

243

322. A rare purple-printed Scottish pottery jug, depicting the popular Victorian singer Jenny Lind, who toured Scotland in 1855. Printed mark 'J. & M. P. BELL & CO' (of Glasgow). *c.* 1855–60.

323. A marked 'Davenport' earthenware dinner plate bearing a rather unusual Continental printed view. *c.* 1845. Diameter 9⅛ inches.

324. An attractive and typical early Victorian wash-basin dish printed with coloured-over fanciful Oriental design 'Canton'. Initial-mark of Robinson Wood & Brownfield, a Cobridge (Staffordshire) partnership of the 1836–41 period. Diameter 12½ inches.

325. A plate from a rare, early multi-colour printed Davenport earthenware service. Impressed 'Davenport' name and anchor-mark with potting date for 1836. Other parts of this set are shown in colour, with the original account in *An Illustrated Encyclopaedia of British Pottery and Porcelain.* Diameter 10¼ inches.

Opposite page

326. A fine and typical early Victorian blue-printed Scottish earthenware water-jug (normally sold with matching basin and sometimes with matching toilet wares). Bearing the initial-mark of R. A. Kidston & Co. of Glasgow. *c.* 1838–46. 12½ inches high.

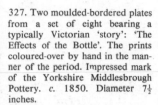

327. Two moulded-bordered plates from a set of eight bearing a typically Victorian 'story': 'The Effects of the Bottle'. The prints coloured-over by hand in the manner of the period. Impressed mark of the Yorkshire Middlesbrough Pottery. *c.* 1850. Diameter 7½ inches.

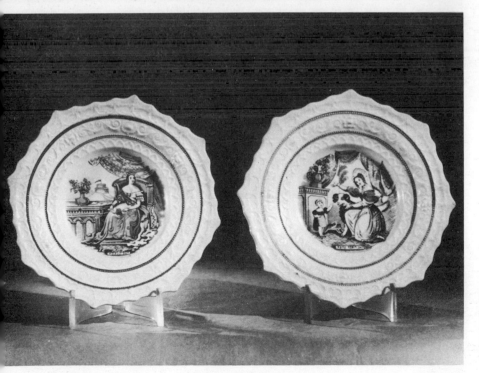

328. Two moulded-edged child's plates of a shape registered in March 1847 by the Staffordshire partnership of Bailey & Ball. This shape of plate—in various sizes—may be found with a variety of naïve but attractive coloured-over prints (see also Plate 329). *c.* 1847–50. Diameter 7¼ inches.

329. An assortment of once-inexpensive mid-19th-century printed (and often coloured-over) earthenwares. The prints depicting typical events or morals (the anti-drink plates shown in the bottom row) of the period. These are folk pottery rather than cabinet pieces but have a charm all of their own, and the range of subject is almost endless. Many different potteries made versions of the popular railway mugs. *c.* 1847–80. 'The Bottle' plate 7½ inches.

Pratt and Colour-printing

In the previous section we have seen mainly simple one-colour printing, and then printed outlines over-painted with colours. We now turn to discuss printing in several colours, a process associated with the Staffordshire firm of F. & R. Pratt & Co., although several other firms used the same technique.

Taking first the Pratt earthenwares, it must be understood that the multi-colour prints did not come into general use until the mid- or late 1840s and that before this, from at least 1810, Felix Pratt had produced at Fenton, in the Staffordshire Potteries, well-printed one-colour useful earthenwares typical of their period. Further, in the 1840s he had introduced a decorative range of Etruscan-styled vases and similar objects, similar to those depicted in the nineteenth-century advertisement reproduced on page 250.

Fine as these Etruscan-design pieces are—having gained the patronage of the Prince Consort—the present-day fame of the Pratt factory has been built upon the reputation of the most humble of objects—pots to contain bear grease, meat, or fish-paste and the like. Not ordinary pots, but ones where the flat, slightly domed cover was used to turn the most utilitarian of articles into a novel object, one of beauty and interest. Here, perhaps, was the earliest use of eye-catching wrapping where the container sells the contents. These decorative colour-printed covers were preserved and became collectable objects, worthy of being framed and hung on a wall, so much so that many persons know only the lids (a typical example is shown in Plate 330), but originally, there was a deep base. Affixing the top to the base and sealing the contents there was glued a printed paper-strip describing the contents and naming the manufacturer. Such a complete pot is shown in Plate 331 while a rarer, tall 'Potted Meat' container is shown in Plate 332.

While we do not know the exact date of the introduction of these colourful printed pots, they were certainly included in Pratt's stand at the 1851 Exhibition. It must be noted, however, that it is unlikely—or at least unproven—that Pratt was the first manufacturer of such wares. What is clear is that he soon specialised in this line and that his examples are, in general, superior to those of his several rivals, the quality of the engraving and the rich colours being superb. Pratt's 1851 Exhibition stand must have been a feast of colour, yet the objects were mere printed earthenware, bearing colourful reproductions of well-known oil-paintings by leading artists—a then novel idea. The 1851 subjects included 'The Last In' after Mulready, 'Highland Music' after Landseer (Colour Plate XI), 'The Blind Fiddler' after Wilkie, 'The Truant' after Webster, 'The Hop Queen' after Witherington (Plate 333), and 'Cottage Children' after Gainsborough. These and other subjects were applied to plates, dishes, and plaques, often furnished with ornate borders.

The selection displayed here tends to neglect the popular pot-lids, but a comprehensive range of these subjects is reproduced in the standard reference-books listed on page 266. Here some of the finer objects are depicted, although some, such as the bottle (Plate 335) bear a pot-lid print re-used on a larger object. The vase shown as Plate 336 illustrates well the quality of the engraving as practiced at the Pratt factory from about 1850. In great measure this is due to the skill of Jesse Austin, an engraver who sometimes added his name or initials to the design. In looking at these patterns—Colour Plate XI for instance—it must be remembered that for each design at least four different copper-plates had to be engraved—one for the basic black outline and detail, then one each to transfer the different colours, normally red, yellow, and blue. Each 'pull' from these plates had then to be correctly 'registered' to give a clear picture with clean outlines.

Many of the popular pot-lid designs and other Pratt colour-printed wares are still quite common and inexpensive, but the several rare subjects, or objects are keenly sought after. Humble pot-lids that originally covered meat-paste are changing hands for over a hundred pounds, for the rarer subjects. All colour-printed Pratt wares are eagerly snapped up (even the comparatively late re-issues made especially for the collectors' market), but there are other types of Pratt earthenware that are most decorative and tasteful and yet are neglected by most Pratt-ware collectors.

I refer, in the main, to the superbly potted terra-cotta wares decorated with tinted, or plain prints. Plates 341–46 show a typical range of such often inexpensive lines, objects that would surely repay collecting. Other types bear prints applied to a pale mauve earthenware body (Plates 347–48), yet other designs are on a white earthenware (Plate 349), while early in the present century a range of objects was ornamented with a matt-black ground silhouetting white classical figure motifs (Plate 350).

№ 340

F&R.PRATT.&C⁰

FENTON

Most Pratt earthenware is unmarked. Some of the 1850 pieces bear a circular printed name-mark, but the pot-lids are, in general, unmarked (except in some cases for Jesse Austin's initials or a registration-mark), as are the mass of pre-1890 wares. After this the name appears more frequently—in the form shown left—with or without the design or border-number, in this case 340.

For non-Pratt colour-printed wares, the reader should turn to page 265.

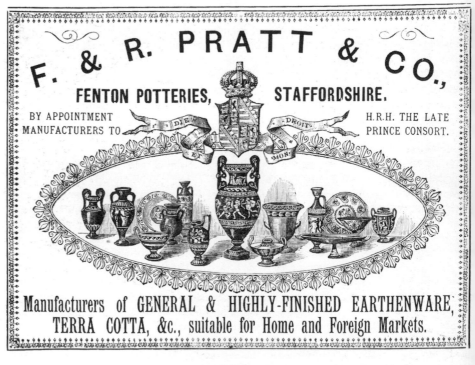

250

330. A well-produced multi-colour printed 'pot lid'. The design was registered on 29 December 1854 in the name of F. & R. Pratt & Co. of Fenton, the best known manufacturer of these popular objects. Diameter 4½ inches.

331. A typical Pratt multi-colour printed bear's-grease pot and cover, as it was sold, with part of the original printed advertising and sealing-band still affixed. In most cases these original bands have been washed away and often even the plain pottery base has been discarded. *c.* 1850–60. Diameter 3 inches.

332. A tall, multi-colour printed F. & R. Pratt covered 'Potted Meat' container, with its original cover. These earthenware pots can be found in a surprisingly large number of different shapes and sizes and with very many different printed patterns—some of which are now very rare. *c.* 1860. 4¼ inches high.

333. A fine, multi-colour, printed Pratt-ware low comport from a dessert service. The centre print is 'The Hop Queen' after the original oil painting by W. F. Witherington. The marbled border is one of Pratt's basic border-motifs. *c.* 1850–60. Diameter 9½ inches, 2 inches high.

334. A small, multi-colour, printed
Pratt-ware plate bearing an 'Interior
view of the Crystal Palace'. Several
Pratt pot-lids and related wares
depict views of the 1851 Exhibition
buildings, or of other later exhibitions. *c.* 1851–60. Diameter 7
inches.

THE QUEEN! GOD BLESS HER!

335. A Pratt-ware, multi-colour printed bottle, one of several characteristic shapes bearing a print also found on pot-lids: 'The Queen, God bless her!' *c.* 1860. $6\frac{3}{4}$ inches high.

336. A superbly engraved design by Jessie Austin; the subject apparently occurs only on Pratt-ware vases of this shape. The print depicts Golden Island, Yangtze River, after T. Allom. *c.* 1860. $5\frac{1}{2}$ inches high.

337. Two Pratt-ware multi-colour printed, floral plates from a dessert service of 'Bouquet' pattern. Several good, printed floral patterns were produced. *c.* 1860–65. Diameter $9\frac{1}{2}$ inches.

338. Two rare and most attractive Pratt-ware jugs, the multi-colour printed dog designs being in this case on a blue ground (other colours occur). These and related prints also occur, rarely, on shaped, oblong, pot-lids. *c.* 1865–70. $8\frac{3}{4}$ and $7\frac{3}{4}$ inches high.

339. An attractive Pratt-ware cup and saucer showing two of several different ruin-subject multi-colour prints. These tea wares and other objects occur with different ground-colours. Marked 'PRATT. 123. FENTON' in three lines. The numbers 123 refer to the border— one which occurs on many objects. *c*. 1880–90. Diameter of saucer $4\frac{1}{4}$ inches.

340. Two scenic-centred Pratt-ware multi-colour printed plates with red border and typical '123' border. These scenic designs can occur with different borders and some examples can be of recent date. *c*. 1910. Diameter $7\frac{3}{4}$ inches.

341. A fine-quality Pratt terra-cotta jug of a characteristic shape. The continuous band printed with a hunting subject. *c.* 1855–65. 6¼ inches high.

342. Two Pratt terra-cotta squat vases of a characteristic form bearing two standard classical figure-subject prints. *c.* 1855–65. 4¾ inches high.

343. An attractive pair of Pratt terra-cotta vases bearing an attractive coloured, printed continuous border—two aspects of which are shown. *c.* 1855–65. 5¾ inches high.

344. A set of three Pratt terra-cotta vases decorated with popular and characteristic printed and coloured border-designs—to be found on many other Pratt objects. *c.* 1865–70. 7 and 4½ inches high.

Opposite page
345. An attractive and well-potted Pratt terra-cotta jug with an unusual printed and coloured Eastern design. This basic shape occurs with many other printed designs. *c.* 1860–65. 5¾ inches high.

346. A handsome and rare Pratt terra-cotta vase of pleasing classical simplicity decorated with a bold, printed, continuous band. *c.* 1860–70. 11¼ inches high.

347. A rare Pratt blue-bodied earthenware-covered oval bowl, printed with a tinted boar-hunting scene. The shape and pattern are unique to F. & R. Pratt of Fenton. *c.* 1857–60. 6 inches long.

348. Three blue-bodied Pratt-ware jugs of a standard shape—here shown in three sizes and showing three characteristic tinted hunting prints. The large jug is inscribed and dated 1859 and is enriched with gilding. *c.* 1856–60. 7½, 6½, and 5½ inches high.

349. A large Pratt earthenware toilet-jug, printed with one of many classical figure subjects—this one was 'registered' in October 1857. 14 inches high.

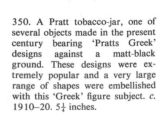

350. A Pratt tobacco-jar, one of several objects made in the present century bearing 'Pratts Greek' designs against a matt-black ground. These designs were extremely popular and a very large range of shapes were embellished with this 'Greek' figure subject. *c.* 1910–20. 5¼ inches.

Pratt-type Wares

As I mentioned on page 249, there were several other manufacturers producing similar colour-printed earthenwares. In fact, Messrs F. & R. Pratt may not have been the first on the market. This honour may well rightly belong to Messrs Thomas, John, and Jos (sic) Mayer of the Dale Hall Works, Longport, Burslem, in the Staffordshire Potteries. This firm's stand at the 1851 Exhibition included: 'Various designs for meat pots, printed in colours, under the glaze ... advertising tiles, of various designs, printed in colours.' These tiles or plaques in particular show the quality achieved by Messrs T. J. & J. Mayer (see Plate 351).

This Mayer partnership traded from 1843 to 1855 and from then on a succession of firms worked the Dale Hall Pottery, each producing multi-colour printed earthenwares. The various firms were:

Mayer Bros. & Elliot	c. 1855–58.
Mayer & Elliot	1858–60.
Liddle Elliot & Co.	1860–62.
Liddle Elliot & Son	1862–70.
Bates Elliot & Co.	1870–74.
Bates Walker & Co.	1875–77.
Bates Gildea & Walker	c. 1877–1880.
Gildea & Walker	c. 1880–85.
James Gildea	c. 1885–88.

Rare examples of multi-colour printed earthenwares occur with the initials of one of these firms according to the date of production, and other examples bear the diamond-shape registration-mark relating to one of the Dale Hall firms. One page from the official records shows the black outline part of two typical pot-lid designs registered by Bates Elliot & Co. on 1 January 1874 (Plate 352). Other shapes, especially the jug shown in Plate 356, were registered by Dale Hall firms and these afford another method of identification. Typical Dale Hall colour-printed pottery is shown in Plates 353–56, but many of the Victorian designs have been produced from the original engraved plates, mainly in the 1950s and early 1960s. These reproductions had tell-tale wording when they left the factory (Plate 360), but subsequently this has often been painted over or otherwise covered!

Several other firms produced colour-printed wares; these include:

Charles Hobson, Albert Pottery, Burslem. c. 1865–75.
Examples bear the 'C. H' initial-marks.

Malcolm & Mountford, Dresden Pottery, Stoke. c. 1862.
Examples bear the name-marks.

Morgan, Wood & Co., Hill Works, Burslem. *c.* 1860–70.
Examples bear the 'M. W. & Co.' initial-marks.

John Ridgway & Co., Cauldon Works. *c.* 1830–55.
These examples are normally in porcelain rather than pottery.

W. Smith & Co., Stafford Pottery, Stockton-on-Tees. *c.* 1825–52.
Examples bear 'W. S. & Co.' initial-marks.

Wood & Baggaley, Hill Works, Burslem. *c.* 1870–80.
Examples bear 'W. & B.' initial-marks.

I hope in this short section to have illustrated the point that not all multi-colour printed earthenware should be called 'Pratt'. The subject is very complex—and therefore interesting. None of the now-available books deal fully with the whole range of products and manufacturers, but regarding the coverage of pot-lid subjects the following works are almost indispensable:

The Pictorial Pot-lid Book by H. G. Clarke (Courier Press, London, 1970).
The Price Guide to Pot-lids ... by A. Ball (Antique Collectors' Club, 1970).
Staffordshire Pot Lids and their Potters by C. Williams-Wood (Faber and Faber, London, 1972).

The reader is also referred to Chapter Six of my *Antique China and Glass under £5* (Arthur Barker, London, 1966). The serious collector should consider joining the *Pot Lid Circle* (Secretary: A. Ball, Esq., 15 Arden Road, Nuneaton).

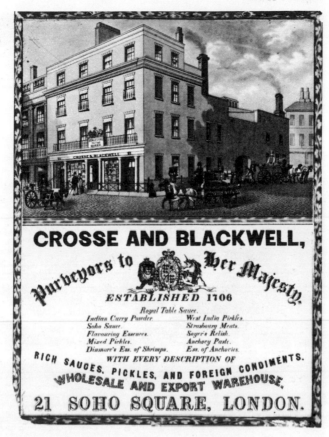

351. A superb Crosse & Blackwell colour-printed advertising plaque, made by Messrs T. J. & J. Mayer of the Dale Hall Works at Longport, a firm which produced a good range of pot-lid-type wares in the style normally attributed to F. & R. Pratt. *c.* 1850–55. 13 × 9¼ inches.

352. Two Bates Elliot & Co. Pratt-type multi-colour printed designs—'Summer' and 'Autumn' (showing the basic printed outline only). This firm was one of several succeeding firms working the Dale Hall pottery and producing Pratt-type wares. These designs were registered on 1 January 1874, and this illustration shows the original designs as submitted to the Design registry.

353. A fine large-size multi-colour printed pot-lid, showing the 1851 Exhibition building. Other Exhibition views were also made. This T. & J. Mayer design was made for Messrs Crosse & Blackwell (see Plate 351). Mayer produced many special containers for Crosse & Blackwell's famous food preparations. *c.* 1851. Diameter 5¼ inches.

354. A superb, large punch-bowl made by T. J. & J. Mayer or one of the later Dale Hall firms. The Bacchus subject border is printed in the so-called Pratt multi-colour technique. Bowls of this type were made in various sizes and can have a simple foot. *c.* 1860–70. Diameter 16¼ inches.

355. Two rare pottery handles printed with two of the popular multi-colour printed shell-motifs. These were made at the Dale Hall pottery and matching finger-plates occur. *c.* 1860–70. Diameter $2\frac{1}{2}$ and $1\frac{1}{4}$ inches.

356. Three jugs of a characteristic Dale Hall shape—registered by Liddle Elliot & Sons on 16 January 1863. Three typical, printed patterns are here shown. Marked with relief-moulded diamond-shaped registration-mark. *c.* 1863–66. $9\frac{1}{2}$ and $7\frac{1}{2}$ inches high.

357. A multi-colour printed earthenware jug, bearing the printed bee- and initial-mark as employed by Messrs Morgan Wood & Co. of the Hill Works, Burslem, during the period 1860–70. 9¼ inches high.

358. A multi-colour printed jug bearing the bee- and initial-mark employed by Messrs Wood & Baggaley of the Hill Works, Burslem, in the 1870–80 period. This design may also have been produced by their predecessors, Morgan, Wood & Co, see above. 9½ inches high.

359. A rare porcelain plate, bearing in the centre a Pratt-type multicolour print normally found on earthenware pot-lids. Probably of Ridgway make (Pratt's head engraver Jessie Austin is said to have been employed by Ridgway's for a period). *c.* 1850–55. Diameter 6¾ inches.

360. The reverse of a post-war re-issue pot-lid by Messrs Kirkhams Ltd. This firm owned the original Dale Hall copper-plates which were not—as claimed—engraved by Jesse Austin who was born in 1806! This tell-tale wording incorporating 'reproduced by . . .' is often painted-over or otherwise covered, but the two pierced holes in the rim do not occur on old specimens.

Majolica Wares

Majolica is, like Parian, a typically Victorian ceramic. The ware was introduced int
England by Minton's famous Art Director, Leon Arnoux, in 1850. He sought to reproduc
the early Continental tin-glazed earthenwares termed 'Maiolica'—with an 'i' rather than
'j'. Many examples, especially the early Minton essays, emulate the true Italian Maiolica i
that the clay-coloured body is coated with an opaque white glaze, totally covering the bas
body. Later in the century the word was applied to a wide range of earthenwares decorate
with semi-translucent coloured glazes (Plates 365, 368–74).

The English Maiolica was first publicised at the 1851 Exhibition where Minton's displa
included a good selection, including the jardinière shown in Plate 361. Other Minto
examples were painted by leading ceramic artists of the period, and the large Continenta
style circular dish or wall plaque shown in Plate 363 is perhaps one of the very fe
examples that can be attributed to Arnoux himself. All hand-painted Majolica is rar
especially the signed examples.

The body quickly caught the public's fancy and numerous manufacturers produced ofte
charming Majolica-type wares with warm-coloured glazes. Many decorative novelties we
made, particularly by the Stoke firm of George Jones. Jones was trained at Minton's b
established his own Trent Pottery in 1861. The George Jones wares were widely acclaime
at the various Exhibitions of the period and include a variety of fancy strawberry-dish
(Plates 371–72) and similar accessories. His examples often bear the impressed monogra
'G J' with, after 1873, '& Sons' added. At its best, Majolica can be very fine and is ofte
underrated, but, as with Parian, many small firms produced inferior examples or piec
made to sell at a very cheap price. The teapot shown in Plate 373 is a typical example of th
class.

Good use was made of Majolica-type coloured glazes on Minton's Art Nouveau-sty
earthenwares early in the present century, see Plates 478–80.

361. An early example of Minton's tin-glazed 'Majolica' earthenware. Purchased at the 1851 Exhibition, one of a 'variety of flower pots . . . coloured in the Majolica style'. 7½ inches high.

362. A finely painted Minton majolica-ware tazza, 'Cupid stealing the thunder from Jupiter' by Thomas Kirkby, an example from the 1862 Exhibition. Diameter 13½ inches.

363. A boldly painted, large Minton Majolica-ware dish with recessed centre. Dated 1859 and signed by Minton's famous Art Director Leon Arnoux. Diameter 17 inches.

364. A Wedgwood Majolica-type earthenware triton candelabra, with tinted glazes. Impressed date-letter for 1869. 12 inches high.

365. A Minton Majolica-ware plateau, painted by Thomas Kirkby and shown at the 1855 Paris Exhibition. Diameter 25 inches.

366. A Minton Majolica-ware figure-supported comport, one of very many table ornaments produced in this style. *c.* 1862. 16¼ inches high.

367. A fine oval Minton Majolica-ware tray, painted, in a typical manner, by Edouard Rischgitz. *c.* 1872. 27 × 16 inches.

368. A George Jones' Majolica-ware comport and a Brown-Westhead, Moore & Co. flower- or spill-vase. Typically Victorian wares still showing charm and decorative merits. *c.* 1880. Comport 9 inches high.

369. A decorative George Jones Majolica-ware individual teaset on tray. A design registered in April 1873. George Jones & Son produced many well-modelled decorative wares in this inexpensive body. Tray 19 inches long.

370. A finely modelled (by J. Henk) Minton Majolica-type hen flower-container, coloured with tinted glazes. The companion cock is shown in colour in the revised edition of Jewitt's *Ceramic Art of Great Britain* (Barrie & Jenkins, 1972). 1875. $12\frac{1}{2}$ inches high.

371. An amusing and decorative George Jones Majolica-type nut-dish. A design registered in December 1869. Length 13½ inches.

372. Another George Jones Majolica-type nut-dish decorated with semi-translucent coloured glazes. Impressed G. J. monogram-mark. *c.* 1870. Length 9¾ inches.

373. A relief-moulded teapot decorated with semi-translucent coloured glazes. A mass-produced, originally inexpensive pot, registered in July 1882 by Messrs Wardle & Co. of Hanley. 4¾ inches high.

374. An unmarked Staffordshire relief-moulded covered cheese-dish, inexpensively decorated with semi-translucent coloured glazes. *c.* 1880–90. 6¾ inches high.

Staffordshire Figures

In using the above description we generally mean nineteenth-century earthenware figures of a simple uncomplicated kind, mass-produced at low cost for the cottage, rather than for the stately home. However, the Staffordshire potters produced in the eighteenth century a spirited assortment of figures, in salt-glazed stoneware (Plates 78–80) and particularly in the Whieldon-type earthenwares, decorated with translucent coloured glazes. We also have the fine-quality models made by the succeeding family of Ralph Woods (Plates 130–31).

Reverting to the nineteenth century, we have those examples decorated with underglaze colours in the manner attributed to the Pratts, but in fact produced by many different potters, several outside Staffordshire. Like most earthenware figures these are unmarked. Plate 375 shows a theatrical figure of this Pratt-type, a remarkable example of the modeller's craft (or craftiness!) for the figure has been simplified to a remarkable degree—the cloak and flowing garment serve to fill the normally troublesome spaces between hands and body or between the legs. This figure could be made from one simple two-piece mould—the potter's delight. The amusing watch-stands shown in Plates 381–82 are other examples of the Pratt-type underglaze colouring.

Other more ornate figures and groups of the early nineteenth century were no doubt made to emulate the slick porcelain examples. These can have a certain charm (Plate 377), but the added 'bocage'—the leafy backcloth—seems out of place in earthenware. With the rather thick opaque overglaze-enamel found on most post-1810 examples of this general type there is a tendency for the enamel to flake, as is seen in Plate 379. The name of Walton is associated with many of these bocaged figures but many other manufacturers made this popular type.

Two features serve to make these originally humble pottery figures charming and collectable. Firstly, their humour (Colour Plate XII) and vigour. Secondly, their historic association, in that the potters caught the market by depicting topical events or endeavoured to depict heroes or heroines of the day, Royalty, theatrical characters, and the like. Many books in recent years have been published on these Victorian portrait-figures and the rarer examples can be extremely costly.

In general, however, the mass of decorative Staffordshire figures—the unnamed lovers and their lasses—are still inexpensive and reasonably plentiful. In fact, few aspects of ceramic-collecting offer more scope for the modest collector, and remarkably little attention has been paid to researching the very many potters who produced these humble wares. The names of only a handful of figure-makers are generally recorded, of these the most famous was Sampson Smith (Plate 399), but the fact that in 1851 this potter only employed ten men, twelve boys, and twenty women and that he described himself as a 'figure manufacturer and beer seller', underlines the modest standing of many Staffordshire figure-makers.

In quality of potting and finish one class stands out supremely, but despite much research we can still not be sure of the firm, or succession of firms, which produced this fine range

The name 'Tallis' (after the source of some theatrical models) is normally given to this class, typical examples of which are shown in Plates 383–85 and 390). But like many other types of Staffordshire figures the moulds have been preserved and twentieth-century examples occur (Plate 400).

Of all the Staffordshire Victorian figure-models, those which have best retained their timeless appeal are the sitting spaniels, examples of which are shown in Plate 394 and in the old photograph Plate 396. These spaniels have been turned out in their tens of thousands up to recent times (although probably none of this type in earthenware pre-dates 1860). Other animal models are even more attractive and much rarer.

This section does not presume to study in depth the figures, the manufacturers, or the production methods, it only serves as an illustrated introduction to a vast subject. The following books will give further guidance:

> *Victorian Staffordshire Portrait Figures for the Small Collector* by B. Latham (Tiranti, London, 1953).
> *Staffordshire Chimney Ornaments* by R. G. Haggar (Phoenix House, London, 1955).
> *Staffordshire Portrait Figures of the Victorian Age* by Thomas Balston (Faber & Faber, London, 1958). (Supplement issued in 1963 by John Hall, London.)
> *Staffordshire Portrait Figures and Allied Subjects of the Victorian Era* by P. D. G. Pugh (Barrie & Jenkins, London, 1970).
> *The Victorian Staffordshire Figure* by Anthony Oliver (Heinemann, London, 1971).

In addition, Chapter 3 of my *Antique China and Glass under £5* (Arthur Barker, London, 1966) is relevant, and useful illustrations are contained in both the *Illustrated Encyclopaedia of British Pottery and Porcelain* (Herbert Jenkins, London, 1966) and my revised edition of *Jewitt's Ceramic Art of Great Britian 1800–1900* (Barrie & Jenkins, London, 1972).

375. A simply-moulded Staffordshire earthenware figure, decorated in the Pratt-style with underglaze colours. *c.* 1810. 6¼ inches high.

376. A typical cow-creamer, as made by many Staffordshire and other potters over a long period in several styles of decoration. These are mostly unmarked and the small lid covering the filling hole in the back is often missing. *c.* 1810. 5½ inches high.

377. Two rare, marked 'TITTEN-SOR' Staffordshire earthenware figures of the 1815–23 period, with typical 'bocages' at the back. 6¾ and 7½ inches high.

378. An impressed marked 'EGYPTIAN PRIESTESS' by 'R^a (Ralph) WOOD. BURLSEM'. This is Ralph Wood III, not one of the two earlier potters of this name (see Plates 130–32). Note the enamel, not translucent, colours. *c.* 1800. 10½ inches.

379. A reasonably common Staffordshire figure of Elijah. Religious figures were popular and made in large numbers. Note the thick, often flaked, enamel colours of the post-1810 period. *c.* 1815–20. 11 inches high.

Opposite page
380. An amusing Staffordshire group relating to 'The New Marriage Act' of 1822. This model has been reproduced at later periods. *c.* 1822–30. 6¼ inches high.

THE NEW MARRIAGE ACT
JOHN FRILL AND
ANN BORE AGED
21 THAT IS RIGHT
SAYS THE PARSON
AMEN SAYS
THE CLERK

381. A charming mantle-ornament, decorated in the Pratt-style with underglaze colours and incised 'J. EMERY. M.BRO (Mexborough, Yorkshire) 1838'. 9 inches high.

382. Two fine and rare earthenware mantle-ornaments, decorated in the Pratt-style with underglaze colours. Perhaps from a Yorkshire factory (see Plate 381) rather than from a Staffordshire pottery. *c.* 1800–1805. 9½ inches high.

383. An imposing and well-modelled Staffordshire earthenware figure, from the so-called 'Tallis' factory. *c.* 1860. 15¾ inches high.

384. A pair of typical 'Tallis' groups of Uncle Tom and Eva, showing the characteristic black-printed quotations. *c.* 1852–60. 8 inches high.

VICTOR EMMANUEL

386. A tall pair of Staffordshire earthenware figures commemorating Queen Victoria's Jubilee in 1887. The male figure is incorrectly titled—a surprisingly common occurence!—and should be the Duke of Edinburgh. *c.* 1887. 17 inches high.

387. A large, unmarked Staffordshire earthenware portrait-figure of the 1885–90 period. A typical example of this once inexpensive class. 18 inches high.

85. A superb Victorian taffordshire portrait-figure of 'ictor Emmanuel', in a dense ody. Note the printed title (see late 384), the modelled front legs compare with the models shown in lates 398 and 399), and the care l manner in which the decora on has been applied. 'Tallis' odels such as this represent the est of Victorian earthenware gures. *c.* 1860–70. 14¾ inches gh.

388. A decorative and rare pair of unmarked Staffordshire earthenware cricketing figures. Several cricketing figures were made and some have been reproduced in recent years. *c.* 1870. 13¾ inches high.

389. A rare Staffordshire earthenware jug in the form of a dressed cat—several such novelties were made. *c.* 1860. 10½ inches high.

390. An elephant mantle-ornament from the 'Tallis' factory. *c.* 1860. 6½ inches high.

391. One of several Staffordshire elephant models; practically the whole range of animal life was depicted. *c.* 1870. 7½ inches high.

392. A rather rare and large Staffordshire earthenware dog model, one of many produced by the Staffordshire figure-makers. *c.* 1870–80. 11½ inches high.

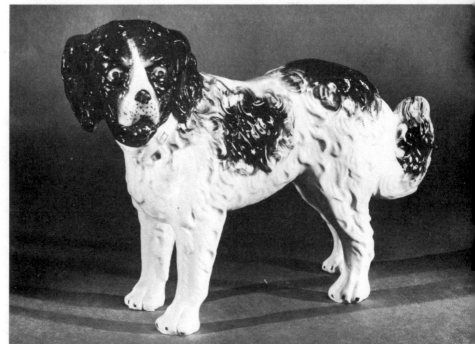

393. A large and rare, free-standing Staffordshire earthenware dog model, perhaps from the Sampson Smith factory. *c.* 1870. 12½ inches long.

394. Two of the everlastingly popular Staffordshire spaniels, which are to be found in differing sizes and styles of decoration. All examples of this model are post-1860, and they can be of quite recent manufacture. *c.* 1880. $10\frac{1}{4}$ inches high.

395. A rare reclining version of the standard Staffordshire spaniel. One of a pair of the 1870–80 period. $9\frac{1}{2}$ inches long.

396. An Edwardian photograph of a paintress decorating Staffordshire spaniels and other standard models. The cat model on the left is rarely found.

397. One of several attractive, but simply modelled (without free-standing feet or other difficult potting features), animal models produced early in the present century by Messrs Charles M. McNay & Sons of the Bridgeness Pottery, Bo'ness, Scotland. Such specimens bear moulded registered numbers such as, in this case, R^d N° 342671. *c.* 1900. $9\frac{1}{4}$ inches long.

398. Two rather poor and 'late' Staffordshire earthenware portrait-figures of Lord Kitchener and General French, but unusual in that they bear the maker's mark SADLER BURSLEM. *c.* 1910. 9¾ inches high.

399. A rare pair of marked 'Sampson Smith, Longton' slip-cast earthenware figures, embellished with post-1880 thin, 'bright' gold which did not need burnishing. *c.* 1890. 13 inches high.

Following page
400. A page from a retailer's catalogue showing 'Reproduction Staffordshire Figures' of the 1910–20 period. Several models are of early 19th-century introduction, such as 'Vicar and Clerk', but these remained popular and the late reproductions are often sold as originals!

REPRODUCTION STAFFORDSHIRE FIGURES.

7681
TOBY CREAM JUGS
Height 3½ in.
2/- each

PEPPER   MUSTARD   SALT   VINEGAR

7618
4 PIECE TOBY CRUET SET
5½ in. high   12/6 set
4½ in. high   9/- set

7999
"SHEEP UNDER TREES"
Height 5 in.
5/6 each

7689
"DEER HUNTERS"
Height 7½ in.
12/- pair

7685
"CAT ON CUSHION"
Height 7½ in.
4/- each

7992
"CLOVELLY DONKEY"
Height 7 in.
7/- each

7727
"FRUIT SELLERS"
Height 5 in.
6/- pair

7682
"VICAR AND CLERK GROUP"
Height 7 in.
21/- each

7683
"INEBRIATE" GROUP
Height 8½ in.
25/- each

7997
"SAMUEL JOBSON AND NELL"
Height 7 in.
14/- pair

7996
"GIN AND WATER" FIGURES
Height 8½ in.
12/- pair

7733
"JUDY" JUG
Height 11 in.
12/- each

7688
"CRINOLINE FIGURE"
Height 8½ in.
11/- each

7993
SHAKESPEARE BUST
Height 8½ in.
13/- each

7680
"PUNCH" JUG
Height 12 in.
12/- each

Doulton Wares

Today the name 'Doulton' is internationally renowned for decorative objects, including fine porcelains made at the Burslem factory, but its beginnings were quite humble. John Doulton (1793–1873) and John Watts traded in partnership as stoneware potters at Lambeth from February 1820 until Watts's retirement in December 1853, and as late as 1847 their typical wares were of a very utilitarian nature. The bill-head reproduced on page 298 lists their specialities, while the written account includes such items as '20 dozen Ginger beer bottles 16/8d'; '2, 4 gallon covered pans 6/–', and '36 gallon bottles 18/–', but interestingly decorative articles were also included: '1 gross whisles 7/6', '3 dozen Bacchus Creams 3/–', etc. Some finely modelled decorative stoneware bottles and a Nelson jug, bearing the standard 'Doulton & Watts' impressed mark of the 1820–45 period, are shown in the *Illustrated Encyclopaedia of British Pottery and Porcelain*, Plate 245. Here, however, we are mainly concerned with the later Henry Doulton period.

Henry Doulton was born in 1820, and in 1835 he commenced his apprenticeship at his father's Lambeth Pottery. In 1846 he set himself up as Henry Doulton to manufacture the then novel and hygenic stoneware water- and sewage-pipes. If Doultons had not progressed to produce any other ware, their contribution to modern drainage and sanitation would have earnt them honourable mention in the history of civilisation. The three separate firms of Doulton & Watts, Henry Doulton & Co., and John Doulton jr. were amalgamated on 1 January 1854 and the new trading style of Doulton & Co. came into being. The staple trade continued to be the manufacture of simple utilitarian stonewares, including the then very necessary and often ornamental stoneware water-filters.

For the 1862 Exhibition Doulton & Co. produced some experimental pieces decorated with incised designs into which blue pigment had been rubbed. These were technically unsuccessful as the colour had fired-out, but the germ of an idea had taken root and the mass of Doulton art-ware that was to be produced at Lambeth in the 1870s through the present century owe their origin to these unsuccessful 1862 trials. Amateur artists from the Lambeth School of Art were taken on to decorate in a simple but powerful manner the simple stoneware forms. These wares were featured in the 1871 and 1872 Exhibitions and were well reviewed in the popular monthly, the *Art Journal*. In an article in the January 1872 issue an interesting note appears, that has some bearing on our appreciation of these wares over a hundred years later:

> With regard to these new products which Messrs. Doulton & Co. have, with such success, brought forward, we understand that should the demand for them increase, it is not their intention to produce them in sets or to make duplicates, in order that the unique character of these products may be sustained; having in prospective the time when such ware may be sought for and gathered into collections and museums.

The engraving shown on page 299 is reproduced from the *Art Journal*'s catalogue of the 1872 Exhibition, but such Victorian engravings do not render justice to the charm of some of the early Doulton decorative stonewares.

Such simple hand-thrown salt-glazed stonewares are best shown in Plates 402–7. Probably the most celebrated of these Doulton stoneware decorators is Miss Hannah B. Barlow (Plate 404), famous for her animal studies, the incised lines being subsequently filled with pigment to accentuate the design according to the depth or thickness of the line. I prefer her earlier work of the 1870s and early 1880s where the border-designs do not overburden the whole (Plate 406) and where simplicity is the keynote, but this artist worked well into the present century, up to 1913. Her work is unique—no two pieces were duplicated, and each example is signed with her monogram. One could usefully note here that Henry Doulton was the first potter to employ female artists and designers and to permit them to sign their work.

Hannah's sister, Florence Barlow, who worked from 1873 to 1909, specialised in a form of cameo-like *pâte-sur-pâte* in which the mainly bird-subjects were built up in slight relief in coloured clays (Plates 408–9). Again each piece is unique and each is signed with her initials F.E.B. in monogram form. These Barlow sisters also had a talented brother, Arthur, and the two early jugs shown in Plates 402–3 are his work. Unfortunately, Arthur Barlow died early in life, in February 1879 and his work for Doulton's is confined to an eight-year period. In recent years, as Doulton's art stonewares have found favour again with collectors after a period of neglect, the ruling prices have increased considerably—especially for the work of the Barlows. This is entirely justified.

While one cannot detail in a general book list, or illustrate, the work of all the many Doulton artists, I cannot fail to mention the talented George Tinworth (see Plate 410). This sculptor's work falls into two categories, his often large-scale monumental groups and his detailed religious subject plaques (Plate 411). However, far more collectable and amusing are his small Lambeth stoneware figures and groups, typical examples of which depict mice or frogs in human pursuits. A selection of these, with a boy musician and a seated figure, is shown in Plate 412. These animal figures are not unique, a popular subject was repeated, but are nevertheless full of vigour and have great appeal. Incised and embossed stoneware vases were also made by Tinworth. George Tinworth's work, up to his death in 1913, is normally signed with an incised monogram of his initials, T G.

There is almost no limit to the range of Doulton wares made from the 1880s to the present century, and while as a class Doulton is plentiful rather than rare, the discriminating collector can find much of real decorative merit. The work of Eliza Simmance (*c.* 1873– 1928) is often very powerful, see Plate 413.

Much of Doulton's Lambeth production was of an architectural nature: much of the Victoria & Albert Museum's ornamental facing is of Doulton make, and a wonderful example of the Art Nouveau style of tiling and decoration can be seen in the Strand opposite the Law Courts, in the entrance to Lloyd's Bank.

In the 1920s Chinese-glaze effects were introduced and proved popular (Plate 416), while in the 1950s Agnete Hoy produced good stoneware designs at the Lambeth works. However, in March 1956 production ceased at this famous pottery and from that date onwards the Doulton porcelains were made in Staffordshire at the Burslem factory, see *British Porcelain: an Illustrated Guide.*

Apart from the Lambeth stonewares featured in this short section, there was also made some fine earthenwares such as 'Lambeth Faience', and other wares were made at the Burslem factory. Samples of later Doulton wares are shown in Plates 550–53, and the reader is referred to Desmond Eyles's book *Royal Doulton 1815–1965* (Hutchinson, London, 1965) for a full account of this important firm.

The basic marks include:—

c. 1870–80	*c.* 1880–1903	*c.* 1872	*c.* 1902–22	*c.* 1922–56

401. An engraving from the *Art Journal* showing Doulton stonewares from the 1872 Exhibition, including Hannah Barlow bird studies.

299

402. An early Doulton stoneware jug made at the Lambeth works. The incised decoration by Arthur B. Barlow. Plated cover. Oval impressed mark with artist's initial monogram A.B.B. *c.* 1870–75. 8 inches high.

403. An attractive and early Doulton stoneware jug made at the Lambeth works and decorated by Arthur B. Barlow. Silver rim marked 1872. Impressed oval-mark and artist's monogram A.B.B. $9\frac{1}{4}$ inches high.

404. An early 20th-century photograph of Miss Hannah B. Barlow in her studio with a partly incised-decorated vase.

405. A charming, early Doulton stoneware jug of unusual form, showing a typical band of Hannah Barlow's incised animals. Oval impressed mark with artist's monogram. *c.* 1872–75. 9 inches high.

406. An early Doulton stoneware vase decorated with Hannah Barlow's incised 'drawings' and showing a restraint of decoration—often lacking on later specimens. Oval-mark with date 1874 and artist's monogram. 11¾ inches high.

407. A typical Hannah Barlow-decorated Doulton stoneware jug. Oval impressed mark with date, 1873 and artist's monogram. 7⅛ inches high.

408. A typical example of Miss Florence E. Barlow's bird studies built up in raised tinted clay. Impressed Doulton name-mark and incised artist's monogram F E B. *c.* 1900. 15 inches high.

409. Three well-decorated Doulton stoneware vases, with raised tinted-clay studies in Miss Florence E. Barlow's characteristic style. Impressed factory-marks and incised F E B monogram. *c.* 1890–1900. $9\frac{3}{4}$ and 14 inches high.

410. A photograph showing George Tinworth working on one of his large-scale groups. *c.* 1910.

411. A framed and glazed example of George Tinworth's religious-subject plaques in terra-cotta, with typical lengthy biblical quotations. *c.* 1890–1900. $17\frac{3}{4} \times 10\frac{3}{4}$ inches.

412. A selection of typical George Tinworth stoneware 'toys'. These, especially the mice and frogs engaged in human pursuits, can be most amusing, and Tinworth recalled that they were carried out as a relaxation and change from his larger serious works. All signed with incised T G monogram. *c.* 1885–1905. 'Play Goers' group 5½ inches high.

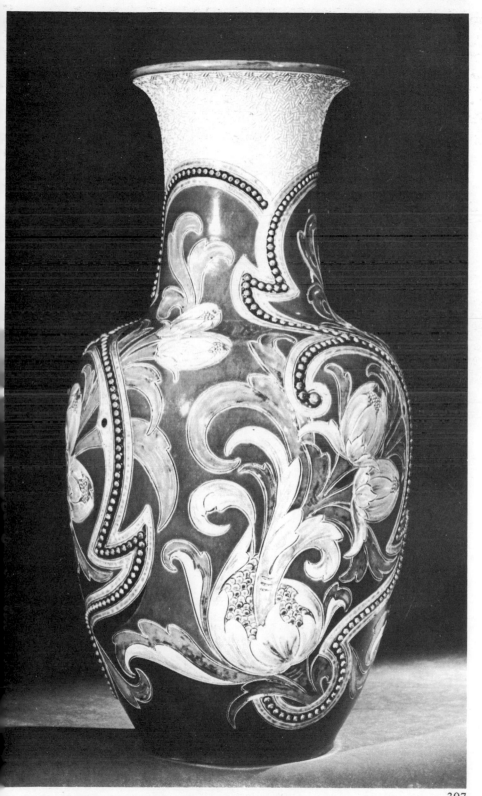

413. A large and forcefully decorated Doulton Lambeth stoneware vase by Miss Eliza Simmance. Impressed mark, with word 'England' added. *c.* 1895–1905. 17½ inches high.

414. Two typical examples of Doulton's Lambeth stoneware modelled by Mark V. Marshall. *c.* 1895–1900. $6\frac{3}{4}$ and $11\frac{1}{4}$ inches high.

415. Two amusing Doulton stoneware pots with hinged covers, bearing impressed design-registration numbers 537199 and 546208 of 1909. $3\frac{1}{2}$ inches high.

416. Two typical examples of Doulton's 'Chang' ware reproduced from a 1929 *Pottery Gazette* advertisement.

417. An example of several commemorative pieces issued in limited editions. This example designed by C. Noke (Art Director) and modelled by H. Fenton was one of two thousand made 'to celebrate the reign of his Gracious Majesty Edward VIII. 1936'. $10\frac{1}{4}$ inches high.

The Martin Brothers

The Martin brothers—Robert Wallace (Plate 419), Edwin, Walter, and Charles Martin— are often cited as the first of the British 'Studio Potters'. They certainly worked as a team producing largely individual wares and carrying out all the various manufacturing processes themselves, from the throwing of the raw clay to the final firing and even the selling of their own wares. Even if other, mainly country, potters had previously been just as self-supporting, the Martin brothers were the first to gain, or seek, national publicity for their novel wares.

'Martinware', as their product is called, is a hard stoneware normally salt-glazed in the traditional manner. It dates from 1873 and for some four years the now-scarce early stonewares were produced at Fulham and bear this London place-name. At first R. W. Martin used Bailey's kiln on the site of the Dwight Pottery (page 53). In 1877 the Martin brothers moved to Southall, and in the following year the Brownlow Street shop (managed by Charles Douglas Martin) was opened, giving rise to the incorporation of the double address 'London & Southall' in the incised name-mark.

The rare, early (pre-1880) wares can be simple and conventional (Plate 418), but the Martin tradition and name was built up on the production of ornately engraved, incised, or carved designs, although the basic vase-forms are good, robust shapes, thrown by Wallace Martin (Plate 425) and seldom embellished with needless handles. Grotesque fish and animal designs are characteristic, but some very good floral designs were incised by Edwin Martin.

Robert Wallace Martin was the sculptor and key figure in the team. He received training at the Lambeth School of Art and at the Royal Academy Schools. From his imagination and hands sprang the famous and now costly two-piece bird and animal models (Plates 426–29). These are useless objects but are full of vigour and are so 'different' as to be remarkable. I say 'useless' but some of these models, such as the bizarre fish shown in Plate 427, are termed 'spoon-warmers'—a use to which they seem rather unsuited. My own preference is for the face-jugs (Colour Plate XIII)—objects later mass-produced by other firms, but here individually made and expressing a lively, mischievous, and happy air. These date from around 1900. The several potting figures and plaques (Plates 422–23) are also very noteworthy and scarce.

After 1900 the Martin brothers simplified their products, and the former scrollwork and grotesque designs gave way to a natural form in a general Japanese style. Plate 432 shows a fine vase in this style dated 1903, while Plates 433–35 show similar wares of the 1907–8 period, reproduced from contemporary sources. Now the glaze seems to have been sparingly applied, if applied at all. At the time of writing (1973) these simple later Martinware designs are unjustly neglected by many collectors, but the scope of the Martin brothers' wares is large, and pieces can be found to suit most tastes.

The year 1910 saw the start of the decline; the Brownlow Street shop was destroyed by

310

fire in that year which also saw the death of Charles Martin. Walter Martin died in 1912 and Edwin, the decorator, died in 1915. The small team could not survive the loss of more than half its number. Robert Wallace Martin lived until 1923, and while some attempts were made to produce, or fire, Martinwares in the 1920s and even later, the story to all intents ends in 1915. In its way, this very talented and individual team of potters made a permanent impression, one that permitted the growth of the twentieth-century Studio Pottery movement. The Martin brothers' individual stonewares are all 'signed', normally with the incised inscription 'R. W. Martin & Bros. London & Southall', together with the date of potting. Some variations in the form of the mark occur, as recorded in my *Encyclopaedia of British Pottery and Porcelain Marks* (1964).

The standard work remains C. B. Beard's now scarce *Catalogue of the Martinware in the Collection of F. J. Nettlefold* (1936), but a brief general account is included in Hugh Wakefield's *Victorian Porcelain* (Herbert Jenkins, London, 1962).

418. A rare, early, and uncharacteristically simple salt-glazed stoneware jug made by the Martin brothers at Southall. Impressed, not incised, mark. R. W. MARTIN SOUTHALL c. 1878–79. 7½ inches high.

419. A photograph dated 1910 showing the Martin brothers in their pottery. From left to right R. W. (Wallace) Martin, Edwin, Walter, and Charles Martin.

Opposite page

420. A rare Martin-ware stoneware vase with decoration incised through a thin, dark slip. An example which heralds the approach of the 20th-century Studio Pottery movement. Dated 7/85 (July 1885) and incised 'Martin Bros, London & Southall'. 8¼ inches high.

421. A robust Martin-ware stone-ware jug with well-controlled incised and coloured decoration. Incised standard mark 'Martin Bros, London & Southall' with date 1/9/81. 1881. 9 inches high.

422. One of several Martin-ware figures depicting potters at work. In this case the thrower, Walter, modelled by R. W. (Wallace) Martin. Signed with initials and dated 11.1900. 6¾ inches high.

423. A Martin-ware relief-modelled plaque showing 'Wheel boy', 'bench boy' (preparing the correct amount of clay), and the 'thrower' at work. *c.* 1900. 16¼ inches long.

424. A Martin-ware vase showing Edwin Martin's speciality of incised decoration. Incised mark 'R. W. Martin & Brothers, London & Southall' and dated 1888. $9\frac{1}{4}$ inches high.

25. Three examples of Edwin Martin's incised decoration on Martin stoneware vases. Each with incised name-mark and dated, left o right, 1889, 1896, 1890. Centre ase $8\frac{1}{2}$ inches high.

426. A rare Martin-ware double-bird group, each with typical detachable head and hollow body. Signed and dated 25/3/1914. 5¾ inches high.

427. A forcefully modelled Martin stoneware fish-spoon-warmer, an object made in the form of many grotesque beasts. Incised name-and-address-mark with date 1895. 10¼ inches long.

428. An unusual version of the standard Martin-ware bird-form covered pot with detachable head. Incised name-and-address-mark with date 1895. 9½ inches high.

429. An early and rather simple version of the almost traditional Martin-ware bird, with detachable head, as modelled by R. W. (Wallace) Martin (see Plate 419). Mounted on original polished wood plinth and with Brownlow Street label, relating to the brothers' retail shop. Incised name-mark and date 21/8/1882. 12 inches high.

430. A spiritedly modelled Martin-ware face jug, dated May 1900. The reverse side is shown in Colour Plate XIII. Incised mark. 9½ inches high.

431. Two typical, early-20th-century Martin-ware face jugs, modelled by R. W. Martin. The smaller one is dated May 1911, the larger is 8¼ inches high and is dated May 1902.

Following page
432. A finely modelled and coloured Martin-ware vase, typical of the natural forms favoured early in the present century (see also Plate 435) and influenced by the work of Japanese potters. Incised mark 'Martin Bros, London & Southall' and dated 1903. 10 inches high.

33. A contemporary, 1907, photograph showing typical restrained Martin-ware of the post-1900 period. All such examples would bear the standard incised name-mark with date of potting.

Reproduced from the *Studio*, November 1907.

321

434. A contemporary 1910 photograph showing typical forms and
simple decoration of that period.
Such pieces are now comparatively
rare.
Reproduced from *The Studio Yearbook*,
1910.

435. A contemporary 1908 phot
graph showing a selection
typical Martin-ware stonewares
the 1905–10 period, displaying t
influence of the Japanese taste f
natural forms.
Reproduced from *The Studio Yearboo*
1908.

William De Morgan

While the Martin brothers whom we discussed in the preceding section were primarily potters, William De Morgan (1839–1917) was a designer and decorator rather than a practical potter. Indeed, many of his blanks were purchased from commercial firms. Nevertheless, his influence was great and today his products are keenly sought after.

William De Morgan was trained at the Royal Academy School and was greatly influenced by William Morris, whom he met in the early 1860s. Originally De Morgan was interested in stained-glass work and by 1869 he was firing his painted tiles at 40 Fitzroy Square, London W.1., but moved in 1872 to Chelsea. For several years his output was confined to tiles powerfully painted in underglaze-blue (Plate 437) and in other colours. Some three hundred standard tile designs were introduced between 1872 and 1882 and many of the original drawings are preserved in the Victoria & Albert Museum.

In the mid-1870s Persian-style designs were introduced both in tiles and in ornamental vases (Plate 438). Good examples in this style can be seen at Leighton House, 12 Holland Park Road, Kensington, London. In 1882 De Morgan moved his pottery to Merton Abbey near Wimbledon, where he remained until 1888. Moving again to the Sands End pottery at Fulham in 1889, he was now in partnership with Halsey Ricardo and they were producing their own vases and other blanks—wares that would bear one of the several impressed factory-marks. The pottery body is lightly-fired, rather granular and friable, far from perfect from a potter's point of view but well suited to the basically ornamental nature of the De Morgan wares and to the broad designs with which they were painted.

The decoration falls into two different categories, the Persian and near-Eastern designs with their seemingly underglaze—or in-glaze colours (Plates 436 and 438) and the lustre-wares. William De Morgan was the first English potter to rediscover the secrets of the antique lustre-effects, and although the result is dependent in the extreme on the variable firing conditions, some superb examples were made (Plates 439–40). The later Pilkington lustre effects (page 361) are related to De Morgan's successful experiments in the nineteenth century.

Much of the sparkle was lost, however, after 1892 when De Morgan was forced by ill health to winter in Italy. He did indeed send designs back to London, but the master hand was lacking, and in 1905 De Morgan retired from the partnership—then comprising himself, Frank Iles, and Fred Passenger. The remaining partners with Charles Passenger continued to decorate blanks in the old style for several years (see Plate 441), and as late as 1921 to 1933 Fred Passenger was decorating De Morgan-styled wares for Mrs Perrin at Bushey Heath.

Apart from the standard factory-marks, the De Morgan wares very often bear the initials of the individual painter; the more important were: Charles Passenger, C.P.; Fred Passenger, F.P.; James Hersey, J.H.; Joe Juster, J.J.

The standard reference-book is *William De Morgan* by W. Gaunt and M. D. E. Clayton-Stamm (Studio Vista, London, 1971), a very well-illustrated book that usefully lists the whereabouts of the main collections of this interesting and decorative pottery.

436. A contemporary 1914 photo-
graph showing typical De Morgan
Persian-style earthenwares dis-
played at the 1914 Paris Exhibition.
Reproduced from the catalogue of the
British section.

437. Three typical De Morgan
tiles. Such objects were the mainstay of the firm and were produced
in great numbers in various
designs. Side examples marked
'D M'
  98 . 6 × 6 inches.

438. A typical William De Morgan pottery vase decorated in the Persian-style. The crazed-glaze is characteristic. Unmarked. 10¼ inches high. *c.* 1880–90.

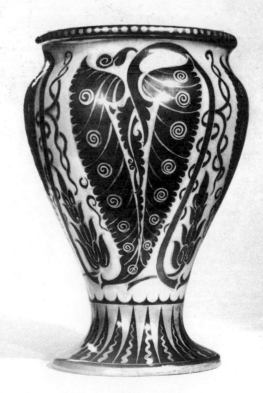

439. A fine, large De Morgan pottery vase decorated with lustre-blue on a cream-ground. Painted mark, 'W. De Morgan. Fulham. F.P.' The initials relate to the decorator Fred Passenger. 13 inches high. *c.* 1890.

440. A fine and typical De Morgan pottery plaque decorated by Charles Passenger in a silvery-lustre on a blue-ground. C. P. initial-mark. Diameter 14½ inches. *c.* 1898–1907.

441. A typical De Morgan-styled bowl made and decorated by Fred Passenger at the Brompton Road workshop between 1907 and 1911 and marked with the initials F.P., also with a printed label—'Guaranteed designed by Wm De Morgan and executed by his original craftsmen'. Diameter 5½ inches.

The Art Potteries

While the Martin brothers and William De Morgan may be considered leaders in the field, there were numerous smaller concerns, usually outside the commercial influence of the Staffordshire Potteries, which produced highly interesting and often very decorative earthenwares. The output of these often little-known potteries offers the discriminating collector great scope, and often good examples can be purchased for pleasingly small sums.

The following twenty pages illustrate typical examples of some of these Art Potteries and the captions or brief textural notes give basic information.

DELLA ROBBIA

The wares here shown in Plates 442–43 are typical examples of the wares made by Harold Rathbone's Della Robbia Company at Birkenhead in Cheshire during the 1894–1906 period. The full name-mark 'Della Robbia' can occur but normally the following device was employed: a third initial was often added above the mast and this relates to the individual artist.

An interesting article on these wares, by Bruce Tattersall, appeared in *Apollo* of February 1973.

LINTHORPE

Linthorpe pottery is of the 1877–90 period; the pottery was established by John Harrison and was at Middlesbrough, Yorkshire.

The original manager was Henry Tooth, later to establish his own Bretby Art Pottery. Many of the Linthorpe shapes and basic designs owe their origin to Dr Christopher Dresser (1834–1904), a designer whose influence is to be seen in several Art Potteries in the third quarter of the nineteenth century. Such pieces often bear Dresser's signature mark, while the standard impressed mark comprises the word 'Linthorpe', often with the outline of a vase superimposed. The conjoined initials HT relating to Henry Tooth were also used as a factory-mark.

Decorative glaze-effects were much used (Plate 445) but hand-painted wares were also made (Plate 446) while typical shapes are shown in the 1889 advertisement.

The Teesside Museums and Art Galleries Service issued in 1970 an interim report on the *Linthorpe Pottery* by J. Le Vine (price 25p plus postage). Information on Christopher Dresser as a designer is condensed in an excellent illustrated catalogue issued by Richard Dennis and John Jesse in October 1972, in connection with their exhibition at the Fine Art Society, London.

442. A selection of Della Robbia pottery reproduced from the *Magazine of Art*, November 1896.

443. An interesting contemporary photograph showing a selection of typical Della Robbia shapes and styles of decoration. Such examples would bear the incised ship-mark. Reproduced from the *Pottery Gazette*, November 1896.

444. An 1889 Linthorpe advertisement showing in engraved form some typical shapes and basic styles of decoration.
Reproduced from the *Pottery Gazette*.

445. A typical Linthorpe pottery vase with streaky glaze. Designed by Dr C. Dresser and marked with signature and Henry Tooth's H.T. impressed monogram-mark. 9 inches high. *c.* 1879–83.

330

446. A boldly painted Linthorpe pottery brown-ground vase, bearing the impressed 'LINTHORPE' name-mark, also Dr Dresser's signature. 9 inches high. *c.* 1879–89.

AULT

William Ault (Plate 447) established his pottery at Swadlincote, near Burton-on-Trent, Staffordshire, in 1887. The pottery produced typical glaze-effect 'Art Pottery' of the period, including several forms by Dr Dresser (Plates 449 and 453), and these examples would bear his name-mark.

The standard factory-mark is reproduced, but a monogram of the initials A.P. also occurs. The pre-1900 Ault-wares are now rather scarce, but the concern continued until 1923 (post-1900 wares are shown in Plates 450, 452, and 475), to be continued as 'Ault & Tunnicliffe Ltd.' (*c.* 1923–37) and to the present time as 'Ault Potteries Ltd.'

447. A contemporary photograph of William Ault admiring one of his Ault-ware vases.

332

448. A selection of Ault-wares shown in this contemporary photograph of a fireplace and overmantle in William Ault's home. The fireplace panels are of Ault ware. *c.* 1900–1910.

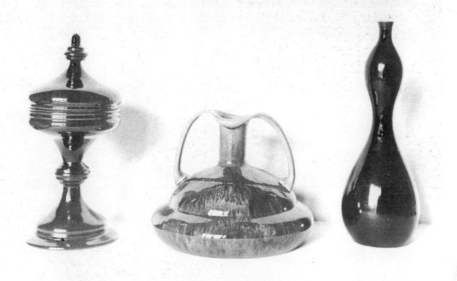

449. A group of three Ault-ware vases designed by Dr C. Dresser and bearing his name-mark. *c.* 1896.

450. A selection of 20th-century Ault-wares showing typical shapes, some designed by Dr C. Dresser. Reproduced from an Ault catalogue.

451. An Edwardian photograph of Miss Gertrude Ault working on a raised-pattern jardinière. Photograph, Miss C. J. Ault.

AULT FAIENCE.

MAURESQUE WARE.

Unique Splashed Striated and Broken Colour
Effects.

Also made in many other Classic Shapes.

452. A selection of 20th-century
Ault-ware vases glazed in the
'Mauresque'-style.
Reproduced from an Ault catalogue.

453. A typical marked 'Ault'
brown-glazed vase after a design by
Christopher Dresser and bearing
his impressed signature-mark. $10\frac{1}{2}$
inches high. *c.* 1890–1900.

Following page
454. A rare Ault Linthorpe-type
pottery vase, decorated with
striated, chocolate-coloured ground
(as Plate 452 shape 271), but bearing the mark 'SALOPIAN' relating
to the Salopian Art Pottery Co., of
Benthall, Shropshire. $8\frac{1}{2}$ inches
high. *c.* 1882–1912.

BARUM, ALLER VALE, AND FARNHAM

'Barum Ware' such as that shown in Plates 455–58 was made from 1879 by C. H. Brannam at his Litchdon Pottery at Barnstaple, Devon. It often displays a quaint charm and the firm, now a Limited Company, continues to the present day. Examples are normally plainly marked and include the trade-name 'Barum'.

The Devonshire Aller Vale Art Pottery wares (Plate 459) of the 1887–1901 period are closely related to the Barum wares, as are also in general effect the Surrey Farnham wares (Plate 460).

BARUM-WARE POTTERY. (English).

An effective highly-glazed Pottery, of English manufacture, novel and quaint shapes. Decorated with raised designs of Fish incised Old English Mottoes, etc., etc., on harmonious toned grounds—some with broad bands in two or three subdued shades, green, brown, cream, blue-grey, etc. Original and artistic.

No. 1. Barum-Ware Jardinieres.
Decorated with broad bands in varied coloured glaze.

3½ inches diameter	Price	1/6 each.
4½ " "	"	2/- "
5½ " "	"	3/- "
7 " "	"	4/- "
8 " "	"	5/- "
Up to 12 inches, Price 15/6.		

No. 2. Barum-Ware Water Sets. (Jug and Two Beakers).
With fish design and Old English mottoes. Rich glazes. Very quaint and novel.
Price—Jugs, 3/6 each; Beakers, 1/9 each.

No. 3 Barum-Ware Vases.
Quaint three-handled vase, with broad bands in subdued glazes.

5 inches high	Price	3/- each.
6½ " "	"	4/3 "
8 " "	"	5/6 "

No. 4. Barum-Ware Flower Holders.
Novel and quaint shape.

6 inches high	Price	1/6 each.
7½ " "	"	2/6 "
11 " "	"	4/6 "

No. 5. Barum-Ware Flower Pot and Saucer.
Conventional glazed fish and wave design, in green on harmonious toned grounds. Very effective and decorative.

5¾ inches high	Price	1/- each.
6½ " "	"	1/6 "
7½ " "	"	2/- "
8½ " "	"	3/- "
9½ " "	"	4/- "

No. 6. Barum-Ware Flower Vase.
With quaint glazed fish design on harmonious toned ground.

8½ inches high	Price	4/6 each.
10 " "	"	15/6 "
12 " "	"	21/- "

With plain bands of colour only.

7 inches high	Price	4/6 each.
9 " "	"	7/6 "

No. 7. Barum-Ware Jugs.
Graceful shapes. Highly effective glazes.

4 inches high	Price	9d. each.
5 " "	"	1/- "
5½ " "	"	1/6 "
6½ " "	"	2/- "

455. An 1898 Liberty & Co. advertisement showing typical Barum-wares, with the basic sizes and retail prices.

456. A further Liberty & Co. advertisement showing Barum-ware shapes and styles of the 1915–16 period.

457. An important Barnstaple incised vase bearing the standard incised mark 'H. Brannam, Barum' with the date 1916. $17\frac{1}{2}$ inches high.

458. A Liberty & Co. advertisement photograph showing typical Barum-ware shapes of the 1920 period.

Opposite page
459. An 1892 Liberty & Co. advertisement showing in engraved form a selection of typical Aller Vale shapes and styles of decoration with the sizes and original retail prices.

ALLER-VALE WARE.

THE ALLER-VALE WARE (made in the West of England) aims at reproducing, with the utmost possible correctness, the effect of Old Rhodian Ware, and is distinguished for its delicacy of colour and quaintness of decoration. The dull brick-reds, soft blues, and deep olives of the Conventional-Floral Designs show to great advantage on the highly-glazed cream grounds. The **Ware** is almost entirely produced by young lads under the direction of Masters, who have made a thorough study of the Old **Moorish** and **Mediterranean** Potteries. The industry is under the direct patronage of H.R.H. the **Princess Louise**, who is pleased to take much interest in the development of the Potteries.

No. 73. **Aller-Vale Jug,** of quaint shape, with slightly marked lip. 7 inches high.
Price **5/-** each.

No. 74. **Aller-Vale Ewer.**
Reproduction of Ancient Persian shape, with large stopper. Suitable for sideboard and over-door decoration.
13 ins. high. Price **21/-** each.

No. 75. **Aller-Vale Flower Pots,** with fluted rims and indented sides. Very practical shapes. The smaller sizes suitable for table decoration.

4 ins. high.	Price **1/9 each.**
5 ″	″ **2/6** ″
6 ″	″ **3/6** ″
7½ ″	″ **7/6** ″

No. 76. **Aller-Vale Plates.**—Very useful for friezes, overmantels, and general decorative furnishing. Broad conventional designs.

8½ ins. diameter. Price **3/6** each.
14 ″ ″ **21/-** ″

No. 77. **Aller-Vale Jug.** Very quaintly shaped, with curious handle, and deeply incurved spout.
8 ins. high. Price **7/3** each.

No. 78. **Aller-Vale Vase,** of Moorish shape, with winged handles. Very effective for overmantel and wall decoration.
8½ in. high. Price **5/-** each.

No. 79. **Aller-Vale Jug.** Tall, slender and graceful shapes. Highly effective for placing on overmantels or sideboards.

4½ ins. high. Price **1/9** each.
6 ″ ″ **3/6** ″
12 ″ ″ **7/6** ″

No. 80. **Aller-Vale Candle-sticks.**
Suitable for overmantels. Very graceful decoration.
7 ins. high. Price **2/6** each.
8 ″ ″ **3/6** ″

No. 81. **Aller-Vale Vase.**
In a variety of shapes, adapted for specimen holders for table decoration.
4 ins. high. Price **1/-** each.

No. 82. **Aller-Vale Vase.**
Slender shape, of characteristic Moorish form.

4 ins. high. Price **1/-** each.
6 ″ ″ **2/-** ″
9 ″ ″ **5/-** ″
13 ″ ″ **10/6** ″

460. A Liberty & Co. advertisement photograph showing typical Farnham-ware pottery of the 1920 period.

461. A contemporary photograph of Edwin B. Fishley (1832–1912) in his Fremington Pottery in Devon. Typical in a general manner of several county potteries, the products of which are now being collected.

RUSKIN

The Ruskin Pottery was established at West Smethwick, near Birmingham, by William Howson Taylor, in 1898. The shapes are generally simple, but some interesting and decorative glaze-effects were achieved (see Colour Plate XIV). Most examples are individual owing to the all-important variations in the kilns.

The standard marks are 'Ruskin Pottery. West Smethwick' within an oval (see Plate 464), and the year of manufacture was often added. Other marks incorporate the word 'Ruskin'. A scissor-like mark was also employed (Plate 467) as was on occasions the name 'Taylor' or a monogram of the initials W.H.T. The Ruskin Pottery was closed in July 1935.

Recently there has been, rightly, a great awakening of interest in Ruskin pottery, with articles in *The Connoisseur* of November 1973 and in *Collector's Guide* of January 1974.

Highest Award. Grand Prize, St. Louis, 1904.

W. HOWSON TAYLOR,

WEST SMETHWICK,
BIRMINGHAM.

SOLE MAKER OF
Ruskin Pottery, Enamels, and Buttons.

Catalogue of the Pottery and Samples of Enamels for Insertion in Metals, Woods, &c., sent on Application.

(Station : SPON LANE (L.N.W.R.) For Dudley trams to Spon Lane.)

462. An early 20th-century Ruskin advertisement showing typical simple bowl shapes, the *Pottery Gazette* advertisement also featuring enamel panels for insertion in woods, etc.

463. A typical and well-controlled Ruskin speckled-glazed bowl. Streaks of purple and black on the sea-green ground. Diameter $8\frac{3}{8}$ inches. *c.* 1910.

Opposite page
464. Two typical Ruskin pottery vases, the up-turned example showing the standard oval impressed mark 'RUSKIN POTTERY WEST SMETHWICK' with the date under 1906. Also a paper label listing awards gained in Milan, St Louis, and Christchurch (New Zealand). 9½ inches and 7½ inches high. *c.* 1906–10.

465. A finely speckled Ruskin pottery vase, black and green on a cream ground. Impressed mark with date 1905. 8 inches high.

466. Three typical Ruskin pottery vases, the contemporary photograph reproduced from the 1913 *Studio Yearbook*.

467. An extremely light and thinly potted, almost egg-shell, Ruskin bowl with typically simple border-motif. Turned to show late painted mark and scissors-mark. Diameter 7 inches. 1922.

BERNARD MOORE

Bernard Moore (1853–1935) was one of England's great ceramic chemists. In 1905 (having previously been connected with the famous porcelain firm of Moore Brothers) he established his own works at Wolfe Street, Stoke-on-Trent, where he specialised in fine glaze-effects (Plate 469), but photographs of such pieces do not do them justice.

Examples are normally signed with the name in full or with the initials B.M. The venture closed in 1915.

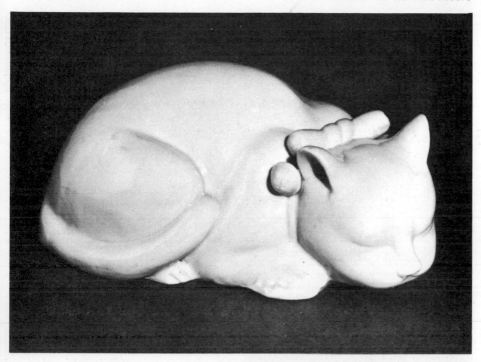

468. A marked 'BERNARD MOORE' copy of an Oriental porcelain cat. *c.* 1910. 6¾ inches long.

469. An important red-ground, marked 'BERNARD MOORE' vase with typical lustre-decoration. Dated, 1908. 12½ inches high.

345

ELTON

Sir Edmund Elton established his Sunflower Pottery on his estate at Clevedon, Somerset, in 1879. After Sir Edmund's death in 1920 the works were continued by his son until 1930. The standard name-mark 'Elton' had a cross added during the 1920–30 period.

470. A typical streaky-glazed Elton-ware vase, with raised motifs, in red, green, and blue. Incised 'Elton' mark. *c.* 1910. 6 inches high.

471. A contemporary 1913 photograph of a selection of typical Coldrum Pottery wares made by R. F. Wells at Chelsea.
Reproduced from the *Studio Yearbook*, 1913.

Art Nouveau

The flowing, florid Art Noveau style was introduced on the Continent in the closing years of the nineteenth century. Typical examples are reproduced in Plate 472, being drawings in a German design-book published in 1899.

The style is mainly reflected in architecture, furniture, metal-wares, and glass rather than in English ceramics; in fact few of the leading British potters and porcelain manufacturers followed the new fashion—probably believing it to be a passing craze. In fact it took a surprisingly long time to pass, its influence being felt up to the outbreak of the First World War in 1914.

The tile-makers were the first of the British representatives of the ceramic industry to follow the lead of the Continental designers, closely followed by the potters concerned in the toilet-ware trade. The advertisement shown in Plate 473 is an interesting and early example of the Art Nouveau 'artistic' designs being reproduced in pottery. The right-hand toilet jug and basin in Plate 474 shows the use of a new artistic printed design applied to an existing old fashioned shape—not a happy marriage.

The new simple shapes are well represented in the 1906 advertisement of Frank Beardmore & Co., but if shown on their own the viewer could well be forgiven for taking these pieces to be of Continental origin.

While in general it was the smaller firms, producing low-price wares, that were influenced by the Art Nouveau movement, one of the large firms in particular took the new fashion as its own and produced splendid examples in tableware. This firm was Minton's, and their Art Director John William Wadsworth (1879–1955) was responsible for some remarkable patterns, such as those featured in the *Studio Yearbook* of 1907 and reproduced here as Plates 477 and 479.

The basic technique was to form in moulds set designs which had low raised walls which served as guides for the decorators and to retain the semi-translucent glazes with which the earthenwares were 'painted'. Such moulded wares could be mass-produced and coloured by semi-skilled labour once the design and the master-models had been made. The vase-forms shown in Plate 478 are typical examples of Minton's twentieth-century Art Nouveau wares—pots that were surprisingly inexpensive. The large dish (Plate 480) is in the same technique, the border including devices reminiscent of the now highly collectable Tiffany glass lamps.

Apart from Minton's, the Doulton potteries produced some good Art Nouveau styled wares, and examples from other firms are shown in Plates 481–83. William Moorcroft's Burslem pottery also shows this influence, and the modern wares made by his son would indicate some rubbing-off of this great decorative fashion of the early 1900s.

Several reference-books give a good general account of the rise and fall of Art Nouveau. Among these we have *Sources of Art Nouveau* by S. T. Madsen (Oslo, 1954), the same authority's *Art Nouveau* (Wiedenfeld & Nicolson, London, 1967), and *The Age of Art Nouveau* by M. Rheims (Thames & Hudson, London, 1966), but none affords very much information on British pottery of the period.

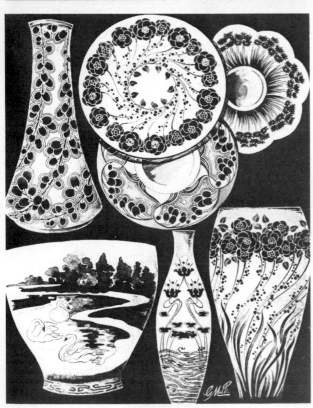

472. Two pages of Art Nouveau style designs reproduced from an 1899 German book, to show the typical flowing lines associated with this period and style.

Greek Shape. Pretoria Pattern, cobalt, finished in gold.

MANUFACTURERS OF
Opaque Porcelain, Dinner, Tea,
Breakfast, and Toilet Ware.

WRITE FOR OUR NEW LIST.

HINES BROS.,
Heron Cross Pottery,
FENTON, STOKE-ON-TRENT.

LONDON SHOWROOMS : 19, THAVIES INN.

Regent Shape. Rd. No. 402,601.
Decoration No. 2,801, cobalt, heavily traced and lined in gold.

474. A *Pottery Gazette* advertisement of 1903 showing typical Art Nouveau-style jugs and basins—a staple line with most commercial pottery manufacturers, tens of thousands of such sets being produced.

473. An Art Nouveau advertisement reproduced from the *Pottery Gazette Diary* of 1901, showing the new fashion and a typical toilet-jug and basin.

AULT FAIENCE.

MAURESQUE
CANDLESTICK.
No. 661.
In two sizes, 6¼ and 8¼ in. high.

ROMAN
CANDLESTICK
No. 393.
9¼ inches high

VASE.

No. 630.
9½ ches high

FIGURED VASE.

VASE.
In three sizes:
B   C   D
8¼   12½   16 in. hi

475. A page from the Ault Pottery
catalogue (see page 332) showing
typical designs of the 1910 period.

FRANK BEARDMORE & Co.
ORIGINATORS AND MANUFACTURERS OF
"THE SUTHERLAND ART WARE"
WORKS: SUTHERLAND POTTERY, FENTON, ENGLAND.

476. An illustrated 1906 advertisement showing Art Nouveau-style 'Sutherland Art Ware'. Such English wares are now quite rare. Reproduced from *Pottery Gazette*, March 1906.

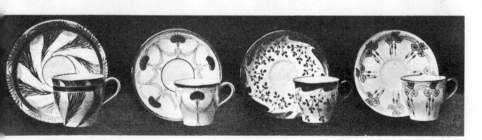

TEA SERVICES DESIGNED BY J. W. WADSWORTH. EXECUTED BY MINTONS, LTD.

477. A selection of Minton cups and saucers designed for Minton's by their famous Art Director, J. W. Wadsworth. Reproduced from the *Studio Yearbook* of 1907.

478. A page from a Minton catalogue of the 1910 period showing typical majolica coloured-glaze designs, as Plates 479–80.

POTTERY AND PORCELAIN

DESSERT PLATES

DESIGNED BY J. W. WADSWORTH,
EXECUTED BY MINTONS, LTD.

479. Two typical Minton majolica coloured-glaze-effect plates designed by J. W. Wadsworth. The flowing glazes are retained by slightly relief-moulded walls. *Studio Yearbook*, 1907.

480. A fine Minton platter decorated with coloured blue, red, and green glazes, within relief-moulded walls. A good example of the Art Nouveau-style of decoration much favoured at Minton's. Date-mark for 1910. Diameter 15 inches.

481. A 'Vana ware' Art Nouveau-style vase produced by Messrs William Bennett of Hanley (1882–1937). *c.* 1900–1910. 8 inches high.

482. A good Art Nouveau-style vase decorated in Minton's technique of coloured glazes within a relief-moulded design. Printed, Thomas Forester & Sons (1883–1959) mark. *c.* 1910. 12 inches high.

483. A simple, inexpensive but imposing marked 'BRETBY' pottery vase with Oriental *cum* Art Nouveau influence. The Bretby wares were made by Messrs Tooth & Co., the Bretby Art Pottery at Woodville, near Burton-on-Trent, Derbyshire. A good range of decorative Art Pottery was produced from 1887 onwards. *c.* 1910. 14¾ inches high.

Maw & Co.

Several potteries, as well as porcelain-factories, were situated in Shropshire. Of the potteries, one of the most important was that of Maw & Co. This concern was established at
Several potteries, as well as porcelain-factories, were situated in Shropshire. Of the potteries, one of the most important was that of Maw & Co. This concern was established at Worcester in 1850 but two years later moved to the Benthall Works, near Broseley in Shropshire.

The speciality of Messrs Maw & Co. was the manufacture of tiles, and after 1861 Maw's made small tesserae from which typically Victorian pictorial mosaics were made up. The business prospered on the manufacture of high-grade decorative tiles (for which in the second half of the nineteenth century there seemed an almost limitless demand) and in 1882–83 new enlarged works were constructed nearby at Jackfield.

While the manufacture of tiles remained the main concern of the firm, some novel decorative wares were made. In particular some vases and ewers were decorated in lustre after the designs of Walter Crane. Typical examples of this rare class are shown in Plates 484–85. Crane and other fashionable designers of the day also designed for this leading firm. Examples are normally clearly marked. After several post-war mergers, the Jackfield Pottery closed in January 1970.

484. A Maw & Co. vase designed by Walter Crane and dated 1899. This firm, famous for its tiles, produced some fine ornamental pottery, see Plates 485–89. 9 inches high.

Opposite page

485. A superb Maw & Co. ewer designed by Walter Crane and painted with gold lustre on a cream ground. Marked 'Maw & Co' with Crane's personal device, a capital letter C with a crane-bird within. *c.* 1885–95. 12½ inches high.

486. A Maw & Co. embossed tile of a characteristic type of the 1905–15 period. 8 inches long.

487. A Maw & Co. printed outline coloured-over pattern after a design by Walter Crane. Marked 'Floriat Maw Salopia'. *c.* 1890. 6 inches square.

488. A Maw & Co. bottle-vase decorated on a cream ground by C. H. Temple, and signed with the initials C.H.T. *c.* 1888. $11\frac{1}{8}$ inches high.

489. A Maw & Co. relief-moulded vase designed by C. H. Temple. Green ground with brown-lustre finish. Dated 1901. $11\frac{1}{4}$ inches high.

Pilkington's Royal Lancastrian

In 1892 the Pilkington brothers built a pottery at Clifton Junction, Manchester. From a modest beginning, the early concern being purely with tiles, one of the most important aspects of twentieth-century decorative ceramics arose. The Pilkingtons employed top chemists, designers, and talented new artists—the leading personality was undoubtedly William Burton (from Wedgwood's), ably supported by his brother Joseph. William Burton was a friend of Bernard Moore and was deeply attracted by this potter's experiments in glaze- and lustre-effects, a facet of ceramic decoration that was to reach its high water-mark at Pilkington's.

Production of tiles started at the new factory on 13 January 1893, and the new wares designed by men such as Lewis F. Day soon achieved renown, being included in exhibitions of the period and publicised in art magazines. Thousands of experiments were conducted by William Burton and his fellow chemists on new glaze-effects, and wonderful results were obtained, so that in October 1903 it was decided to embark on the manufacture of decorative glazed ornamental wares. In November of that year Lancastrian pottery was born. Abraham Lomax, one of Burton's team, has written:

> In June 1904, the first examples of the ware were publicly exhibited. The exhibition caused quite a sensation among potters, connoisseurs, lovers of art and of beautiful pottery, and also the general public. The shapes were true pottery-shapes, characterised by simplicity and directness, without twisted handles or other abnormalities. The thrown pots appeared to be the natural outcome of spinning clay on a revolving table with the workman's hands in control. . . .

These early wares were decorated only with mottled and opalescent glazes without painted designs, the mark (when one was used) is the single initial P.

The most famous of the Pilkington decorative achievements are the iridescent lustre-effects, which have been likened to all the iris-colours of a soap bubble, painted on various coloured grounds. Typical specimens are shown in Colour Plate XV and in Plates 492–99. Experiments on these metallic lustres commenced in 1903, and by the time of the Franco-British Exhibition of 1908 the Pilkington Lancastrian wares had won international repute. Now-famous ceramic artists and designers were employed and each signed his work with a personal monogram, a table of which is reproduced. Some designs were the work of Lewis F. Day or Walter Crane and their marks occur also on such pieces, together with the impressed factory-mark. The two basic types of mark are reproduced. Below this would be impressed the year in Roman numerals during the period 1905–13, i.e. VIII for 1908.

The Pilkington lustred earthenwares were somewhat costly, for they were largely individual hand-painted designs in a technique full of difficulties: the firing temperature and atmosphere had to be exact for the iridescent lustres to mature and for the colours to be clear and pure. A piece fired to perfection in every part is a rarity. Often one side or part is

c. 1904–14

c. 1914–35

361

affected to some degree by firing hazards and the sheen or colour will be dull or almost fired-out.

In 1913 H. M. King George V granted the prefix 'Royal' to the company and the wares were henceforth known as 'Royal Lancastrian'. During the 1914–18 war two talented artists left the firm—C. E. Cundell and Gordon Forsyth. In 1915 William Burton left, and for the next twelve or so years the firm traded on its name without the introduction of new effects. In 1928, however, 'Lapis Ware' was introduced. In this, underglaze colours subtly intermingled with the covering semi-matt glazes. These wares are of good, uncluttered shapes, having a certain boldness of treatment that is appealing (Plates 500–501). They were introduced, however, during the Depression, and these relatively costly, sparsely decorated, pots did not find general favour at the time. In September 1937 it was decided to close the Royal Lancastrian Pottery, the last firing being in March 1938.

Much attention has rightly been paid to the fine lustre-designs, and good examples are now costly. In contrast, little attention has been paid to the later wares, those designs depending on surface-texture and line, and shapes that are perhaps timeless (Plate 503). Other designs of the 1930s were impressed or incised, and some of the animal-motifs by Richard Joyce are forceful. A representative selection of the later Royal Lancastrian pottery shapes and basic styles of decoration is shown in Plates 504–7, being reproductions from the company's catalogue of the mid-1930s.

At all periods the Pilkington Lancastrian pottery is uniquely interesting and decorative, and always of fine quality. It represents one of the last efforts to produce individually designed patterns in commercial quantities. In collecting terms it has distinct possibilities. The standard work on the subject is *Royal Lancastrian Pottery, 1900–1938*, privately published by the author, Abraham Lomax (formerly chemist to the company) in 1957. Good articles on this pottery have also appeared in the following magazines:

Apollo, October 1961, article by G. A. Godden.
Spinning Wheel (U.S.A.), March 1970, article by Chester Davis.
Connoisseur, May 1970, article by Miss L. Thornton.
Collector's Guide, September 1973, article by A. J. Cross.

Examples are also illustrated in exhibition-catalogues such as that of the 1914 Paris Exhibition and in *Studio Yearbooks* of the period (see Plates 490–93, 498). Specimens can be seen in the Victoria & Albert Museum in London and the Whitworth Art Gallery (University of Manchester) and at the Manchester Art Gallery at Wythenshawe Hall. The name is continued today in the trading-style 'Pilkington's Tiles Ltd.'

LEWIS F. DAY
Designer

R. JOYCE

JESSIE JONES

G. M. FORSYTH

GWLADYS RODGERS

WALTER CRANE
Designer

C. E. CUNDALL

ANNIE BURTON

W. S. MYCOCK

DOROTHY DACRE

THE "PEACOCK FEATHER"
DESIGNED BY J. CHAMBERS

THE "BIRD AND CHERRY TREE"
DESIGNED BY C. F. A. VOYSEY

THE "BIRD AND VINE"
DESIGNED BY C. F. A. VOYSEY

Previous page

490. Three Pilkington tile-designs reproduced from the *Studio Yearbook* 1906, showing designs by J. Chambers (left) and by C. F. A. Voysey.

491. Three Pilkington vase-forms, decorated with typical streaked glaze-effects.
Reproduced from the *Studio Yearbook*, 1906.

492. A selection of Pilkington lustre-wares: the leopard vase, centre right, is by Richard Joyce, the other designs by Jessie Jones.
Reproduced from the *Studio Yearbook*, 1909.

"THE GREEN SEA."   "THE PERSIAN BOWER."

493. Two Pilkington covered vases, decorated with bright, lustrous colours by Richard Joyce.
Reproduced from the *Studio Yearbook*, 1911.

364

494. A fine Pilkington ruby-ground lustre dish painted by Richard Joyce, *c.* 1910. Diameter 14¾ inches.

495. A selection of typical Pilkington lustre-ware with fine, bright colouring and lustre. Left vase by G. M. Forsyth 1908, centre vase by W. S. Mycock 1923, 8½ inches high, bowl painted by Mycock after a design by Walter Crane, 1912.

496. An imposing Pilkington charger, painted by Richard Joyce in silver lustre on a blue and green ground after a design by Walter Crane. Dated 1907. Diameter 19¼ inches.

497. A selection of Pilkington lustre-wares. From left to right, by M. S. Mycock 1924, Mycock 1911, Mycock 1908, C. E. Cundall 1908, and G. M. Forsyth 1907. 8 inches high.

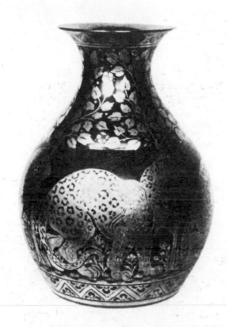

498. A selection of Pilkington lustre-vases each painted by the animal-specialist Richard Joyce. Reproduced from the *Studio Yearbook*, 1914.

499. A fine and typical Pilkington lustre-vase painted by Richard Joyce on a deep blue ground. *c.* 1912. 10½ inches high.

500. A typical Pilkington 'Lapis ware' vase of the early 1930s painted in brown by Gwladys Rodgers. 7½ inches high.

501. Two typical Pilkington incised and moulded vases of the early 1930s. The lion vase in orange and brown, the floral vase in turquoise and deep blue. 8½ and 9¾ inches high.

502. Two Pilkington pots decorated with a mottled-orange ground.
Reproduced from *Our Homes and Gardens*, December 1923.

503. A selection of typically simple Pilkington wares of the mid-1930s. Thrown by E. T. Radford and bearing his initials. Centre vase $6\frac{3}{4}$ inches high.

504. A selection of Pilkington 'Lapis-wares' of the mid-1930s, showing typical shapes and designs.
Reproduced from the firm's catalogue.

505. A further selection of Pilkington 'Lapis-wares' with some relief-moulded designs reproduced from a catalogue of the mid-1930s.

506. A selection of Pilkington
'Lapis-wares' reproduced from a
catalogue of the mid-1930s.

507. A selection of Pilkington
wares of the 1930–38 period,
decorated in black, orange, and
vermilion.
A page from the firm's catalogue.

Moorcroft

WILLIAM MOORCROFT

The designs and pottery of William Moorcroft (1872–1945) are rightly highly commended, and in 1972 the Victoria & Albert Museum celebrated this potter's birth with a special, and revealing, exhibition of his work. Moorcroft came of a potting and artistic family, and after training at the South Kensington Art School he returned to Staffordshire, where from 1898 he was employed by Messrs James Macintyre & Co. Ltd. of Burslem. This firm produced mainly utilitarian earthenwares (see my *Illustrated Encyclopaedia of British Pottery and Porcelain*, Plates 364–65), but William Moorcroft was concerned with a then-novel range of decorative 'Florian' wares, in which the mainly floral designs comprised relief or slip-trailed outlines, into which the appropriate colour was added. The beaker illustrated in Plate 510 illustrates the style and technique very well.

Such wares proved very popular, and the bold signature 'W Moorcroft' appears on each piece, together with the standard Macintyre printed mark—a rare early instance of the designer's name being credited.

In 1913 William Moorcroft built his own relatively small factory, the Washington Works, at Burslem. Pottery in the former Macintyre floral style was produced, the design becoming simpler and bolder as time progressed (see Plate 512), and landscape-designs were also produced using the same trailed-outline technique. Other fine and decorative glaze-effects were successfully experimented with (Plate 508), an example of which is the speckled-blue glaze on 'powder-blue' tablewares, one of the staple lines that has proved so popular over many years. The shapes (Plate 514) were brilliantly simple and then novel, being, like some Wedgwood designs, almost timeless and nearing perfection.

In 1928 William Moorcroft was appointed potter to Queen Mary, a fact recorded in marks from this period. While the traditional floral patterns were produced in the 1930s, some delightfully simple wares were made—a selection is seen in Plate 515. After William Moorcroft's death in October 1945, his eldest son Walter (Plate 516) continued the Moorcroft tradition, designing each new shape or decorative motif employed on these characteristically handsome wares.

Richard Dennis, the London dealer, issued in 1973 an excellent and well-illustrated exhibition catalogue on William Moorcroft's life and work; this is a most useful reference book.

508. A 1921 photograph showing
William Moorcroft with a selection
of his vases.
Moorcroft family photograph.

509. A James Macintyre & Co. marked vase, decorated (and signed) in William Moorcroft's typical style. Dated 1913. $9\frac{1}{4}$ inches high.

510. A typical James Macintyre & Co. three-handled cup, decorated by William Moorcroft and bearing his signature-mark. *c.* 1910. $4\frac{3}{8}$ inches high.

Hand-painted in shades of deep blues and greens upon a groundwork of rich grey-blue, with the surface enriched by a translucent overglaze of soft yellow.

No. 1.
FLOWER POTS.
3½ ins. diameter, 5 6
5½   ,,   13 6
7½   ,,   27 6

No. 2.
TOBACCO JARS.
4½ ins. high, 10 6
5½   ,,   12 6

No. 3
FLOWER VASES.
4 ins. high, 4 9

No. 4.
VASES.
For cabinets.
6½ ins. high, 8 9
9   ,,   16 6
13   ,,   28 6

No. 5.
FLOWER VASES.
For sideboards and tables.
3½ ins. high, 5 6
4½   ,,   12 6

No. 6.
VASES.
For overmantels and cabinets.
6 ins. high, 7 6
9   ,,   16 6
12   ,,   22 6

No. 7.
BEAKER-SHAPED VASES.
6 ins. high, 4 9
8   ,,   7 3
10   ,,   11 6
12   ,,   17 6

No. 8.
VASES.
6½ ins. high, 6 9
12   ,,   22 6

No. 9.
BEAKER-SHAPED VASES.
8 ins. high, 11 6
10   ,,   15 6
12   ,,   18 6

512. A selection of typical Moorcroft shapes and styles of decoration. The central vase (12½ inches high) is a Macintyre example, the others post-1913 Moorcroft productions.

513. A set of Macintyre vases decorated by William Moorcroft and bearing his signature-mark. *c.* 1910. 8 and 8⅜ inches high.

511. A Liberty & Co. advertisement of *c.* 1914 showing a selection of Moorcroft's 'Hazledene ware' and the continuation of the Art Nouveau influence.

451. Hot Water Jug.
½ pint .. 3/6
¾ pint .. 4/-
1 pint .. 4/6
1½ pints .. 5/-
2 pints .. 5/6

452. Jug.
1 pint .. 2/9
2 pints .. 4/-
3 pints .. 6/3
4 pints .. 6/9

453. Hot Water Jug.
½ pint .. 3/6
¾ pint .. 4/-
1 pint .. 4/6
1½ pints .. 5/-
2 pints .. 5/6

455. Cream Jug.
2¼ ins. high. 1/9
2½ ins. high 2/-

456. Cream Jug.
2¼ ins. high 2/-
3 ins. high 2/3

457. Sugar Bowl.
3/-

458. Butter Dish.
4/9

459. Broth Cup.
3/3 and 4/3

460. Salt Bowl.
1/3 and 1/6

461. Egg Cup.
1/1

454. Plates.
5 ins. diam. 1/3
6 ins. diam. 1/6
8 ins. diam. 2/-

462. Coffee Pot.
½ pint .. 4/-
1 pint .. 4/9
2 pints .. 6/6

464. Coffee Pot.
½ pint .. 4/-
¾ pint .. 4/6
1½ pints .. 5/9

465. Bowl.
2/- and 2/3

463. Bowl.
6 ins. diam. 2/3
7 ins. diam. 3/3

466. Egg Cruet.
Complete 3/3

467. Preserve Jar.
3½ ins. high.
3/3

468. Cruet Set.
Complete .. 8/9

469. Butter Dish.
3 ins. high .. 4/-

470. Coffee Cup and Saucer.
2/3

471. Breakfast Cup and Saucer. 3/-
Tea Cup and Saucer.
2/3

472. Tea Pot.
½ pint .. 3/- 1½ pints .. 4/6
1 pint .. 3/9 2 pints .. 5/-
3 pints .. 6/9

473. Muffin Dish.
6/6

474. Tea Pot.
½ pint .. 3/- 1½ pints .. 4/6
1 pint .. 3/9 2 pints .. 5/-
3 pints .. 6/9

514. A Liberty & Co. advertisement of the early 1930s showing a selection of Moorcroft's famous powder-blue table wares. Such wares were made over a long period.

515. A selection of simple William Moorcroft wares, reproduced from the *Pottery Gazette Diary* of 1935.

516. Walter Moorcroft, the son of William, seen showing the paintresses how to decorate the blanks. The traditional Moorcroft style has changed very little over the past fifty years.
Pottery Gazette photograph.

'Cheap Lines'

In the preceding pages I have shown articles that can reasonably be regarded as tastefully designed and the product of care and expertise. Such wares were relatively expensive and were sold only at the better-class shops or stores. They were purchased by a relatively small proportion of the buying public. For every Moorcroft or Pilkington vase that was sold, a thousand or more inexpensive sets of vases were sold to those buyers who demanded show and bulk for a shilling or two, or even for pence.

Sample illustrations are here given, showing typical examples of the lines popular in the early years of the present century. These illustrations are taken from contemporary advertisements in the trade journal, *Pottery Gazette*. The objects are of slip-cast earthenware—light in weight and bearing coloured prints, also often bearing signatures such as 'Kauffman', to give the appearance of hand-painted objects. Many of these inexpensive pieces were unmarked. The original caption to the photograph here numbered Plate 519 read:

CHEAP LINES in Vases, Salads, Fruits, Marmalades, Biscuit jars, Moustache [cup or mug], Nutbowls, Clock sets, Trinkets, Candlesticks, Sweets, Flowerholders, &c.
Assorted £5 sample crates of these goods showing all varieties can be packed from Stock . . .

The clock sets must have been sold in hundreds of thousands. In their way they were obviously a commercial success and they have given pleasure to their owners.

Many other 'cheap lines' found a ready market. The Staffordshire figures (page 296) continued to sell in the present century, although after 1910 very few, if any new models were introduced. Nevertheless, the manufacturers continued to produce ever-popular images from the existing moulds. The spaniels proved especially popular and their appeal seems as timeless as the Willow pattern.

Other popular lines included Willow-pattern wares, flower-pots and jardinières in countless variety, cheese dishes (Plate 520), toilet-jugs and basins in profusion (Plate 521). Water- and milk-jugs were also made in their tens of thousands and sold for a few pence.

Mention must also be made of the mass of foreign 'cheap lines' that flooded into this country—the 'early to bed' type of small porcelain group—souvenirs inscribed with the names of various resorts—pictorial plates—candlesticks—cheese dishes. The list is endless, but in general, the imports were of porcelain rather than earthenware.

This brief section has been included to show the complete picture—the bad as well as the good—or rather, the cheap as well as the costly, but although we may wish to belittle these 'cheap lines', they are typical of their period. They have been little researched, but of late some collectors have turned their attention to these wares, and in time to come they may find their place with now revered ceramics.

517. A 1921 advertisement photograph relating to Messrs Aynsley & Fell Ltd, Royal Art Pottery, Longton, Staffordshire, the 'largest makers of flower-pots and clock sets in the World'.

518. A detail from a 1910 advertisement of the 'Royal Art Pottery Co', Waterloo Works, Longton. 'Vases in endless shapes, sizes and decorations, clock sets in countless sizes, shapes and decorations. . . .'

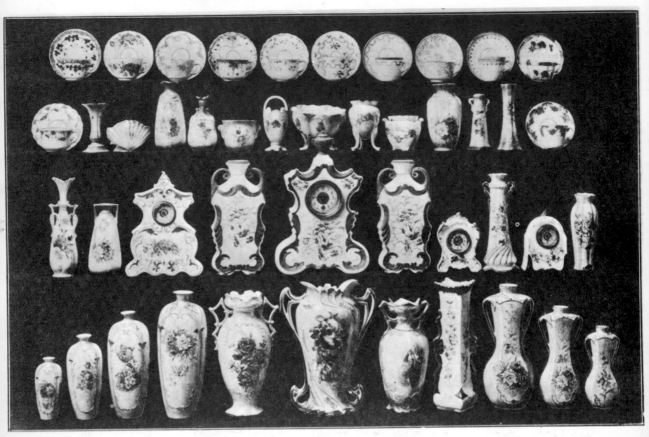

519. A detail from a 1906 advertisement of Messrs Thomas Poole, Cobden Works, Longton. 'Cheap lines in vases . . . clock sets, trinkets, flower-holders, etc.'

Right
520. A Grimwades advertisement of 1906 featuring a selection of inexpensive cheese-stands ('20 well assorted for 30/–') a very popular Edwardian 'cheap line'.

Following page
521. A Wagstaff & Brunt (1880–1927) advertisement of 1905 featuring typical 'cheap lines' including toilet-sets—ewer, basin, chamber, soap, and brush stand at 2/9 per set!

'Cheap Lines'

GRIMWADES, Ltd.

WINTON, STOKE, and ELGIN.

Potteries: STOKE-ON-TRENT.

NEW CHEESE STANDS.

20 DIFFERENT SHAPES.

"NORFOLK" SHAPE.

"ADAM" SHAPE.

"SHELL" SHAPE.

"BYRON" SHAPE.

ALL ARTISTIC AND UP-TO-DATE.

A 1 VALUE— EXCELLENT DECORATIONS.

"PEARL" SHAPE

"TOKIO" SHAPE.

"OCEAN" SHAPE.

"DOROTHY" SHAPE.

A LOT OF 20, WELL ASSORTED, FOR 30/-.

TRY A SAMPLE LOT.

WRITE FOR NEW CATALOGUE.

GRIMWADES, Ltd., {WINTON, STOKE & ELGIN.} Potteries: STOKE-ON-TRENT.

COMPLETE PRICE LIST, Containing **500** *Illustrations and Lithographs sent free on application.*
Please mention " POTTERY GAZETTE."

TOILET SETS, DINNER SETS, TEA AND BREAKFAST SETS, TEAPOTS, VASES.

COVERED CHEESE STANDS, SETS OF JUGS, FLOWER POTS, and all kinds of General and Decorated China and Earthenware for Home and Export.

TOILE? SETS—Consisting of 1 Ewer, 1 Basin, 1 Chamber, 1 Open Soap and Brush Vase, *2/9 per Set.*

WAGSTAFF & BRUNT,

RICHMOND POTTERY, LONGTON, STAFFORDSHIRE.

Art Deco and the 1920s and 1930s

The term 'Art Deco' arose from the 1925 Paris Exposition des Arts Décoratifs. 'Modernist' was a description much used, and here in general the designs are chunky and angular in contrast to the flowing lines of Art Nouveau (page 347) but the two descriptions are now somewhat loosely applied to all the novelties of the 1920s and early 1930s.

The designs of the late Miss Clarice Cliff typify the period, and the names of two of her popular designs, 'Bizarre' and 'Fantasque', aptly sum up many so-called Art Deco objects. We are here concerned with earthenwares, but it must be remembered that related designs are to be found in all mediums.

Allowing for the fact that these wares are comparatively modern, they are quite scarce and little serious study has been applied to this period. However, in regard to one designer, Miss Clarice Cliff, we have the benefit of her own writings. After showing an early inclination for art work Clarice Cliff joined the staff of Messrs A. J. Wilkinson Ltd. of the Royal Staffordshire Pottery at Burslem, a firm that had also acquired the adjoining Newport Pottery Company. Miss Cliff relates how the new designs were introduced:

The warehouses of the Newport Pottery Co. were stacked with bowls, vases, jugs and candlesticks, mostly of the Art Nouveau period. This huge stock had always interested me and presented a challenge. Eventually about 1924–5, I was allowed to experiment. First, with one or two girls who had learned how to use the decorator's wheel, round shapes were covered from top to bottom with coloured bands. . . . Between guide lines they drew simple diamonds which in turn were filled in with bright colours by other girls . . . a sizeable amount of goods were accumulating. These were a source of much merriment and derision to the travellers, to whom the idea of having to offer for sale so much crude colour, after selling only traditional prints and lithos, was a shock. However, after much persuasion the largest car on the factory was filled with a representative assortment and to their amazement it was quickly sold and within two days they were back for more.

We progressed to circles and squares and simple landscapes—all within the operatives' capabilities. These cried aloud for shapes other than the traditional and so the conical shape was evolved. As we grew, so did the number of shapes [early shapes and designs are shown in the contemporary advertisements shown in Plates 522–23] and the number of boys and girls we trained increased to about three-hundred. We were copied by so many that we had eventually to patent [register] many shapes. Even the Japanese copied some!

. . . After a few years all the making was transferred to the Royal Staffordshire Pottery and the whole of the Newport Pottery was taken for the decoration of 'Bizarre' ware. There was one large department for the decoration of Crocus, the Ravel and other popular designs. Some customers preferred modern shapes and patterns, others

385

liked traditional shapes and modern patterns . . . . The the war came and the army, munitions, mines etc. claimed all our workers except one girl who was a semi-invalid.

These Wilkinson earthenwares designed by Clarice Cliff are praiseworthy in many respects, they are gay and colourful and typical of their period. An exhibition of these wares was held at the Brighton Museum and Art Gallery in 1972 and the array was truly breathtaking. It is noteworthy that at first once unsaleable stock was resurrected and made ultra-modern by the application of basically simple designs that inexpensive semi-skilled labour could master. Yet, how much better are these clean designs than the lifeless printed Willow-pattern-type printed earthenwares. In some respects, however, the novel shapes can be faulted—try cleaning the interior of the teapot shown in Plate 524. Also the early cups had solid handles that became very hot and gave no finger-hold, but these defects were soon rectified by opening or piercing the handle.

The patterns were widely advertised under the designer's name—an uncommon practice—and each of the several different printed marks employed, incorporates a facsimile of Clarice Cliff's signature, normally with the name of that particular pattern.

Apart from these simple Clarice Cliff designs, the Wilkinson Company also produced earthenwares painted by leading artists of the period, such as Dame Laura Knight, Sir Frank Brangwyn, and Vanessa Bell.

Other typical 'Art Deco' type wares of the 1930s are shown in Plates 527–32, being reproduced from *Pottery Gazette* trade advertisements, as stated in the captions. Other wares of the period depended mainly on the line for their effect, for example the pieces designed by Keith Murray for Wedgwood's and shown at the 1935 English Pottery Exhibition (Plate 534). The Wedgwood vase shown in Plate 533 is a powerful but simple design, typical of this period. In general, however, this firm was more concerned with pieces of traditional Jasper wares, and these 'modern' shapes of the 1930s are rarely met with.

STILL GROWING in STYLE and SALES.

522. A detail from a 1930 A. J. Wilkinson Ltd. advertisement showing the novel 'Bizarre' shapes.

"Bizarre" and "Fantasque" by Clarice Cliff.

"BIZOOKA"

A. J. WILKINSON Ltd. Newport Pottery Co. Ltd.,
Royal Staffordshire Pottery, Burslem.

523. A detail from a 1929 Wilkinson advertisement showing the new Clarice Cliff designs.

524. Clarice Cliff-designed Wilkinson tea wares potted in August 1930 and bearing the printed marks 'Hand-painted Fantasque by Clarice Cliff. Wilkinson. England. Registration applied for'. Teapot $4\frac{3}{4}$ inches high.

525. A typical Clarice Cliff plaque, 18 inches in diameter and a small vase, marked 'Clarice Cliff, Fantasque, Wilkinson Ltd'. *c.* 1930–35.

526. A typical Art Deco-style low vase designed by Clarice Cliff, and a tall vase showing the earliest type of landscape-design—as Plate 524. *c.* 1930–35. Tall vase 8¾ inches high.

527. A selection of Art Deco-style wares reproduced from a Wade Heath & Co. Ltd. *Pottery Gazette Diary* advertisement of 1936.

Opposite page

528. A James Sadler & Sons Ltd. advertisement showing novelty teapots of the 1938 season. This Staffordshire firm has produced literally millions of teapots since 1899.

529. A detail from a 1935 New Pearl Pottery Co. Ltd. *Pottery Gazette* advertisement featuring its 'Royal Bourbon Ware' in the style of the Clarice Cliff designs.

530. A detail from a 1935 John Beswick *Pottery Gazette* advertisement showing typical so-called Art Deco wares.

531. A detail from a 1933 Thomas Forester & Sons Ltd. *Pottery Gazette* advertisement, the wares reflecting the broad Art Deco-style of the period.

Crown Devon

S. FIELDING & CO, LTD
DEVON POTTERY, STOKE-ON-TRENT.

(above) This vegetable dish and plate are taken from a dinner service which has a particularly neat floral design —a combination of beauty and utility.

(below) A hunting motif provides the source of decoration for this lamp and cigarette box. On pressing a button, the latter slowly opens and closes to the tune of " John Peel."

(above) This vase and fruit dish depict the modern trend in matt glazed pottery. An original colour scheme is carried out in fawn mocha -brown, pale orange and gold.

(below) Three more novelties to amuse your friends. A musical cigarette box, which delivers the cigarette through the dog's mouth, and a musical jug and mug, which on being lifted, tinkle out a well-known tune.

(above) A morning set such as this, in a delightful colour scheme of pale blue, green and pink, would be a very welcome sight first thing in the morning. The tray holds all the pieces compactly and serves as a saucer for the cup.

532. A 1937 S. Fielding & Co. Ltd. *Pottery Gazette* advertisement showing a selection of 'Crown Devon' wares in the style now termed 'Art Deco'.

533. A smart and unusual Wedgwood Art Deco vase, gilt on a deep chocolate-coloured ground. *c.* 1935. 12 inches high.

534. A selection of Wedgwood wares designed by the firm's famous designer Keith Murray and shown at the 1935 English Pottery Exhibition. *c.* 1935. Basalt vase $6\frac{3}{4}$ inches high.

POOLE

Among the other earthenwares of the 1930s, a vast field of which only isolated parts can be covered here, we find standing almost alone the opaque-glazed Delft-like Poole pottery. This is normally decorated in broad designs, muted in comparison with the Clarice Cliff patterns. The atmosphere of Poole pottery of the 1920s and 1930s is suggested in Plates 535–39. All such pieces are hand-painted, and this Dorest firm continues to the present time making a large range of useful and ornamental wares.

535. A detail from a 1923 Poole Pottery advertisement appearing in the *Pottery Gazette Diary*, showing typical products of the period.

536. A detail from a 1931 Poole Pottery advertisement appearing in the *Pottery Gazette Diary*, showing typical products of the period.

537. Two typical floral-painted Poole Pottery vases of the mid-1930s, each glazed with the characteristic matt-white glaze. Impressed mark 'Carter Stabler & Adams Ltd. Poole. England'. $4\frac{3}{4}$ and $3\frac{1}{2}$ inches high.

538. Poole Pottery wares as featured in the *Studio Yearbook* of 1924, showing typical shapes and designs of the period.

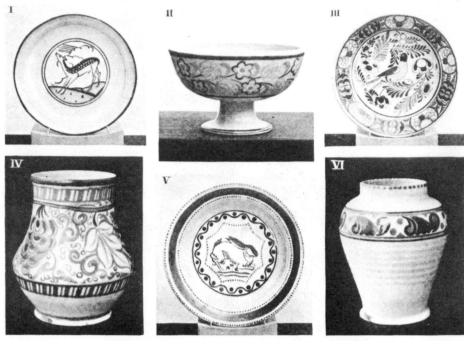

I, II, III, IV AND VI PAINTED POTTERY; V SLIP-PAINTED DISH, DESIGNED BY TRUDA ADAMS AND EXECUTED BY CARTER, STABLER AND ADAMS, POOLE, DORSET

539. Poole Pottery wares as featured in the *Studio Yearbook* of 1926, showing typical designs by John and Truda Adams.

I. AND V. PAINTED DISHES DESIGNED BY TRUDA ADAMS
II. POT GLAZED IN EGYPTIAN BLUE BY JOHN ADAMS
III. PAINTED PLATE DESIGNED BY TRUDA ADAMS
IV. AND VI. PAINTED POTS DESIGNED BY TRUDA ADAMS
POTTERY EXECUTED BY CARTER, STABLER AND ADAMS, LTD., POOLE, DORSET

Following page
540. A fine stoneware group of mother and child by Phoebe Stabler, the wife of Harold Stabler of the Poole Pottery. Both Harold and Phoebe Stabler modelled figure and other wares; examples are normally signed and dated. This is dated 1911. 8 inches high.

POWELL DECORATED WEDGWOOD

A noteworthy feature of the mid-1920s was the popularity of simple, often cottagy, hand-painted designs. At Wedgwood's Staffordshire factory Alfred and Louise Powell decorated the simple Wedgwood creamwares. They also trained women painters to decorate these by hand. The table wares shown in Plate 543 are typical and were featured in a 1928 *Connoisseur* advertisement. The Powells built up a similar reputation to that enjoyed earlier by Emile Lessor—Mrs Powell was, in fact, his grand-daughter. Exhibitions of their work were held and several private commissions were undertaken. One such special order is illustrated in Plate 542, a large bowl made for John Masefield, inscribed and dated May 1926. The Powell monograms are:—

 Personal mark of Alfred Powell *c.* 1904–39.

 Personal mark of Louise Powell *c.* 1906–39.

Several designs feature lustre-decoration but the work of these two artists was quite limited, and signed pieces are rarely found.

541. Three Wedgwood creamware bowls decorated in London by Alfred H. Powell.
Reproduced from the *Studio Yearbook* of 1908.

542. An important, inscribed and dated Wedgwood footed-bowl, decorated by Alfred H. Powell and signed with his AP monogram. Inscribed 'Painted for John Masefield by Alfred Powell, May, 1926'. $13\frac{1}{4}$ inches high.

GROUP OF POTTERY DESIGNED AND PAINTED BY ALFRED H. AND LOUISE POWELL

LARGE LUSTRE VASE DESIGNED AND PAINTED BY LOUISE POWELL

543. Wedgwood hand-painted creamwares in the Powell tradition, reproduced from *The Connoisseur*, September 1928.

544. Wedgwood creamwares decorated in London by Alfred and Louise Powell and bearing their monogram-marks.
Reproduced from the *Studio Yearbook* of 1915.

GWENDOLEN PARNELL

Just as hand-painted earthenwares held their own with mass-produced printed wares, so a market was built up for hand-made figure-models, expensive compared with the factory products but having individuality. Two typical, but rather modest, examples by Gwendolen Parnell are shown in Plates 546–47. Miss Parnell worked at Chelsea and her figures bear the incised mark 'Chelsea-Cheyne' with the year of production added. She had a team of female helpers and her own work is marked with her initials and a drawing of a rabbit. The working period of this Chelsea venture is 1916–36, but this talented modeller also worked in porcelain for the Royal Worcester Company.

545. Three Gwendolen Parnell Chelsea Pottery figures exhibited at the British Industries Fair and featured in the *Studio Yearbook* of 1919.

546. A typical 'Chelsea Cheyne' figure of the 1920s as produced by Gwendolen Parnell between 1916 and 1936. Dated 1925. 7¼ inches high.

547. Another typical incised-marked 'Chelsea Cheyne' pottery figure by Gwendolen Parnell. These were very often mounted on a wood plinth to overcome the troublesome warping of the pottery base. Dated 1923. 7 inches high.

CHARLES VYSE

548. A selection of Chelsea pottery figures by Charles Vyse. One is up-turned to show the characteristic monogram-mark C V with the date 1921 and place-name 'Chelsea'. These moulded figures are very well decorated and are very decorative and typical of their period, but they are not unique—many were produced of the more popular designs.

Also at Chelsea at the same period, Charles Vyse was producing slip-moulded figures displaying fine modelling and good decoration. These figures have not the life of the hand-built Parnell examples, but they are most decorative and typical of their period. The basic mark of the CV monogram above the place-name 'Chelsea' is shown with representative figures in Plate 548, and it can be seen that the year of manufacture is normally added to the mark. Charles Vyse turned from this type of pottery-figure in the early 1930s and concentrated on his famous stonewares (Plates 565–66).

HENRY PARR

Yet another Chelsea artist, Henry Parr, made a limited range of pottery-figures during the 1919–40 period. His 'Primavera' is shown in Colour Plate XVII, a model signed 'Hy Parr. Chelsea. 1935'. It is suggested that these present-century Chelsea earthenware figures are well worthy of attention; at present they are known only to a few devoted collectors, who will surely reap good rewards.

While most of the leading pottery-manufacturers tended to leave the figure market to the porcelain-makers—both English and foreign—there were notable exceptions and a charming Wedgwood model is shown in Plate 549.

Other typical designs of the 1920s and 1930s are shown in Plates 550–54. The rather chunky teapot (Plate 551) is a Doulton product, after a design by the famous artist (Sir) Frank Brangwyn R.A., although the 'Brangwyn Wares' bear little relation to this artist's other works.

549. A powerfully modelled Wedgwood pottery figure of the 1920s or early 1930s. New Wedgwood figure-models are rare, the firm still being largely concerned with the traditional jasper-wares. $14\frac{1}{2}$ inches high.

550. A Doulton stoneware three-handled loving-cup made at the Lambeth works and dated 'Xmas 1925'. 7 inches high.

551. A Royal Doulton (Burslem) earthenware teapot, one of a range of wares designed by the famous artist Frank Brangwyn R.A. and marked to this effect. *c.* 1930. 6½ inches high.

552. An inexpensive, but charming, Royal Doulton flower-bowl of the 1930s. Standard printed mark. 4¾ inches high.

553. An unusual Royal Doulton 'Titanian ware' oval teapot decorated in mottled grey, blue, black, and green. c. 1935. 5½ inches high.

CORONATION WARES

The rather charming child's teaset showing H.M. Queen Elizabeth II as a baby illustrates not only typical shapes of the period but also leads us to discuss coronation wares, in particular those pieces made to commemorate the coronation of King Edward VIII. Because of the abdication before the coronation, many persons believe that their examples of such commemorative wares are of extreme rarity—even unique! This is far from the case because most of the manufacturers had already produced in tens of thousands their souvenirs and had even advertised their own particular designs (Plate 555). Warehouses were packed with such objects which were later sold off extremely cheaply. These Edward VIII coronation wares were therefore made in quantity ready for the market which collapsed overnight and they were in general not sold to the public until some thirty years after the event they were to commemorate. Most coronation wares were mass-produced and decorated by printing processes, but some of the larger firms produced good-quality limited issues inscribed to this effect; some firms even produced commemorative tiles (Plate 556).

Soon after the outbreak of the 1939–45 War production of British ceramics for the home market was savagely curtailed. Factories were taken over for war work and trained personnel were drafted to the Services or were employed on armaments and other essential work. Pottery was extremely scarce, and what was available was of a utilitarian nature and normally undecorated. In contrast to the home-market wares, efforts were made to produce decorative goods for export, particularly to the United States of America, where valuable dollars were earnt by these products. A selection of recent British pottery is featured in the last section of this book, see page 424.

The general background to this period and its decorative arts is covered in two well-illustrated books by Martin Battersby, *The Decorative Twenties* and *The Decorative Thirties* (Studio Vista, London, 1969 and 1971).

H.R.H. PRINCESS ELIZABETH
BORN APRIL 21ST 1926.

OUR EMPIRE'S LITTLE
BORN APRIL 21ST 1926.

SOUVENIR
OF
PRINCESS ELIZABETH
· BY ·
SPECIAL PERMISSION
OF HER ROYAL HIGHNESS
THE DUCHESS OF YORK.

554. A charming child's teaset depicting H.R.H. Princess Elizabeth after a photograph by Marcus Adams. Marked 'Reproduced by Paragon China Co. England. By Special permission of H.R.H. Duchess of York'. *c.* 1928. Teapot 7½ inches long.

555. Detail of a 'New Chelsea' advertisement in the *Pottery Gazette Diary* of 1937, showing wares made to commemorate the coronation of King Edward VIII.

556. A rare 1937 coronation tile made by Messrs Marsden Tiles and inscribed on the reverse 'May 12th, 1937'. 8¼ and 6¼ inches.

Studio Pottery

To many people the description 'Studio Pottery' indicates modern, individually made wares, but if we accept as a working definition that Studio Pottery is made by one man, or a small team, carrying out all the different processes, from preparing the basic materials to the final firing, and that this same person also shapes and decorates the object to his own design, then this takes us back into antiquity and most pre-1750 English earthenwares, certainly the slip-decorated wares (Plates 2–23) fall into this category.

The Studio Potters, as we accept the term today, came into being in the second half of the nineteenth century when the commercial potters were intent on enlarging their factories to mass-produce endless lines of monotonously similar, impersonal objects showing little or no clay-feeling. To fill this void and their own sense of achievement came such potters as the Martin Brothers (page 310) with their lively stonewares. Happily, some large firms also saw the light and encouraged individual artists to work their own designs; the Doulton stonewares can perhaps be termed Studio Pottery (see Plates 402–9), although people such as George Tinworth (Plate 410) were employed by a very large concern and drew a regular wage. Today, some firms—for example, Poole Pottery and Wedgwood's—also have separate studios where individual wares are made.

The Martin Brothers' stonewares attracted much publicity, as did the individual De Morgan wares and the Doulton stonewares, so that talented persons were attracted to the craft of pottery-making as a means of expression and a source of livelihood. These craftwares of the 1900–1920 period are a very mixed bag—some very amateurish—but the best gradually made itself evident and established a standard. With Studio Pottery, individual taste is all-important. Such a potter ideally makes what he (or she) likes, rather than what the buying public may require. Here perhaps lies the essential difference between the commercial manufacturer and the Studio Potter. In practice, however, there has to be some compromise, for the Studio Potter and his family have to live! Very many potters have relied on part-time teaching as a means of making a living.

As individual taste plays such an important part in this aspect of pottery, there are widely differing opinions on the merits of the various wares and, of course, the taste of the 1920s (with wares in general emulating early Oriental styles, see Plates 558 and 561) is not necessarily the fashion today. Plates 567–77 show some of the pieces I admire, for differing reasons. These range from the world-renowned work of Bernard Leach to potters with only a very local reputation. For my own taste I require Studio Pottery to be hand-thrown on the potter's wheel and to be simply decorated. My own preference is for robust stoneware, showing the texture of the body. My ideal is expressed in the stoneware vase shown in Plate 572, a pure shape without painted embellishment, but many recent products are of a totally different nature, not to my taste, but expressing the maker's personality and the time in which it was made.

Although names and period are given in the captions to the illustrations, I do not wish to enter into personalities in this section—rather to keep to generalities, leaving the taste of the reader to find its match in the work of one or more of the hundreds of potters practicing their craft in Great Britain today.

My own field of collecting is large, but of all the types I acquire, Studio Pottery gives me the most satisfaction. One is buying a creation because one admires its line or decoration, not because it is old (age is a dubious attribute). One can discuss the object with its maker and one is helping to support a traditional craft.

Each district has its Studio Potters. These should be sought out and supported, if only by encouraging the local museum curator to build up a small representative collection. Several books are available to give guidance on pottery craft. Some of these are listed below and should be in most libraries, but a practical appreciation of the basic techniques and difficulties of pottery can best be achieved by attending even a brief course such as is given by several Art Colleges or Colleges of Further Education. Several working potters also run summer schools and the knowledge gained through any of these classes will materially help one to understand and appreciate the varying merits of all types of pottery, whether it be antique or modern.

Some of the following books deal with the techniques of pottery rather than with the work of potters, but all books by practising potters are of interest, as they explain not only methods but also the potter's aims.

Handcraft Pottery by Henry and Denise Wren (Pitman, London, 1928).
20th Century Ceramics by G. Forsyth (Studio, London, 1936).
The Art of the Potter by D. Billington (Oxford University Press, 1937).
A Potter's Book by B. Leach (Faber & Faber, London, 1940).
Craftsmanship and Design in Pottery by W. B. Dalton (1943).
The Art of the Potter by W. B. Honey (Faber & Faber, London, 1946).
The Modern Potter by R. G. Cooper (Tiranti, London, 1947).
The Work of the Modern Potter in England by G. W. Digby (Murray, London, 1952).
Artist Potters in England by M. Rose (Faber & Faber, London, 1955—2nd revised edition 1970).
Stoneware & Porcelain, the Art of High Fired Pottery by D. Rhodes (English edition, Pitman, 1960).
The Technique of Pottery by D. Billington (Batsford, London, 1962).
Practical Pottery & Ceramics by K. Clark (Studio, London, 1964).
The Art of the Modern Potter by T. Birks (Country Life, London, 1967).
Pottery in Britain Today by M. Casson (Tiranti, London, 1967).
Bernard Leach, a Potter's Work by B. Leach (Evelyn, Adams & Mackay, London, 1967).
Pioneer Pottery by M. Cardew (Longman, London, 1969).

While no book at present lists the many hundreds of past and present Studio Potters (which omission I hope to rectify), my *Encyclopaedia of British Pottery and Porcelain Marks* (Herbert Jenkins, London, 1964) does list the marks and working periods of very many of these individual potters.

Many shops display a range of modern Studio Pottery, but a particularly good assortment can be seen at the retail showrooms of the Craftsmen Potters Association, William Blake House, Marshall Street, London W.1, and the author, at the time of writing, hopes to display a selected range of individual pieces at Geoffrey Godden, Chinaman, 17–19 Crescent Road, Worthing, Sussex.

557. A photograph of the Maidstone (Kent) Studio Potter, John Solly throwing a simple vase-form on a potter's wheel.

558. A selection of British Studio Pottery of the 1928 period. No. 1. W. Staite Murray, 2 & 3 Bernard Leach, 4 & 5 T. R. Parsons of the Yellowsands Pottery, Isle of Wight. Reproduced from the *Studio Yearbook*, 1928.

Opposite page

559. A selection of early Leach pottery table wares, simple robust forms that set a high standard and gained much publicity for the Studio Pottery movement. Reproduced from the *Studio Yearbook* of 1929.

Following page

560. A fine Bernard Leach vase acquired for the Victoria & Albert Museum in 1931. 10½ inches high.

(1) STONEWARE BOWL, BY W. STAITE MURRAY, 13, WICKHAM ROAD, LONDON, S.E.4 ; PARCHMENT GLAZE, WITH FREE BRUSH DECORATION IN LUSTROUS PURPLE-RED ; (2) and (3) STONEWARE POTTERY BY BERNARD LEACH, ST. IVES, CORNWALL ; *left*, COVERED POT, RUST AND BLACK BRUSH WORK ON WHITE GROUND ; *right*, ELEVEN SIDED BOWL, MATT CELADON. (4) AND (5) STONEWARE POTS BY T. R. PARSONS, YELLOWSANDS POTTERY, BEMBRIDGE SCHOOL, ISLE OF WIGHT

Stoneware by BERNARD LEACH, The Leach Pottery, St. Ives, Cornwall. (Photographed for " The Studio" by Maurice Beck and Helen Macgregor.)

561. A fine Bernard Leach vase in the Oriental taste. Marked with personal 'B L' seal and St Ives pottery seal. *c.* 1930. 8 inches high.

562. A Bernard Leach vase with deep-green glaze and simple incised decoration, marked with personal 'B L' seal and St Ives pottery seal. *c.* 1930–35. 7 inches high.

563. A photograph of W. Staite Murray (*d.* 1962) decorating a vase, with finished vases on the bench. *c.* 1950.

564. A W. Staite stoneware bowl of Oriental simplicity, marked with 'M' seal. *c.* 1952. 3½ inches high.

565. A photograph of Charles Vyse of Chelsea in his studio decorating a stoneware vase. *c.* 1955.

566. A selection of Charles Vyse stonewares in the Oriental taste. All signed 'Vyse' and dated 1936, 1937, or 1938. Large vase of 1936, 9¾ inches high.

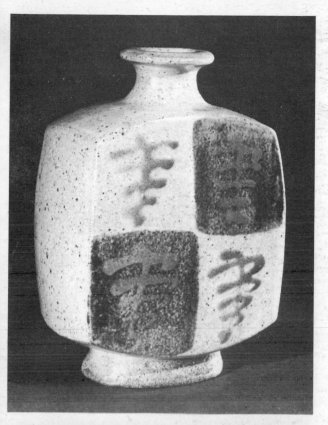

571. An imposing stoneware vase by Hans Coper and marked with his 'H C' monogram. *c.* 1968. Photograph, the British Council.

Previous page

567. A Bernard Leach stoneware vase of 1964 vintage, bearing his personal seal and that of the St Ives pottery. 7½ inches high.

569. A neatly potted and attractive covered stoneware bowl by Katharine Pleydell-Bouverie. *c.* 1930. 6¼ inches high.

568. An imposing Bernard Leach vase with Tenmoku glaze. The 'B L' personal seal and the standard St Ives Pottery device is also shown. 1964. 12¾ inches high.

570. A handsome and workman-like slip-decorated stoneware pitcher by Michael Cardew of Winchcombe. Purchased for the Victoria & Albert Museum in 1938. 11⅜ inches high.

572. A simple, but noble, stoneware vase by the Sussex potter Ray Marshall. Incised full signature with date 1961. 12 inches high.

Following pages

573. A finely potted celadon-glazed stoneware vase by the Staffordshire potter Derek Emms. 1962. 15 inches high.

574. A brown-glazed stoneware vase by Michael Buckland of the Green Dene Pottery, Surrey. 1965. 8¼ inches high.

575. A selection of stonewares of the early 1960s by, from left to right, Helen Pincombe, Daphne Henson, and Eleanor Whittall. Vase 9½ inches high.

576. British Studio Pottery of the mid-1960s by, from left to right, Muriel Wright, Paul Barron, Annette Fuchs, and Vera Tollow. Large vase 10 inches high.

577. A selection of finely potted stonewares of the early 1970s by David Leach, son of Bernard Leach. Since 1956 David has worked at his own Lowerdown Pottery, Bovey Tracey, Devon. Covered bowl 4½ inches high.

578. An amusing, original wall-panel by the Sussex potter Raymond R. Everett. 1971. 24 × 16 inches.

579. A stoneware bowl with wax-resist border-decoration, by Douglas Thornton. 1970. Diameter 7 inches.

580. A stoneware cooking-pot made at the Mag-Mell Pottery, Shalesbrook, Sussex. 1972. 6½ inches high.

581. Two stoneware flower-containers from the Val Barry Studio Pottery, London N.8. *c.* 1972.

582. Modern stoneware by Colin Kellam of Totnes. 1971.

Modern Commercial Pottery

In this final section we move on from mainly individual Studio Pottery to the mass-produced factory-made wares. Whilst the Studio Potters make mainly, but not exclusively, container wares such as vases and bowls, the commercial potter relies for this staple trade on table wares—dinner, tea, and coffee services. Such items as dinner plates, each to an exact pattern, are best suited to factory production-lines rather than to the potter's wheel, and here it is a matter of deciding which articles are best adapted to the different manufacturing processes.

Modern British pottery can be conveniently grouped into two classes. Firstly, the traditional designs and shapes, as produced by such firms as Mason's Ironstone China Ltd. (see also page 204), examples of this firm's products being shown in Plate 599. Many persons tend to criticize such traditional designs, but they sell and sell well in many overseas markets, as well as at home. They have an old world charm and warmth that is lacking in many modern 'clean' designs. Such firms are merely making wares that have stood the test of time and are producing what they make best and what they have a market for. To many people such designs speak of old England (although in many cases the designs have an Oriental origin) and their lives would be all the sadder for the loss of such traditional wares.

Secondly, and in contrast, we have the clean modern shapes and designs. Wares well suited to modern flats, to modern living, and dish-washers. The 'oven to table' wares are a great boon, as well as being attractive. Here the potters are fighting off the advances of the heat-proof glass oven-wares. While one must admire many recent designs, they tend to lack warmth and often nationality. This is not surprising, for they are often intended to be international and are the work of international designers. For example, the new 'Kiln'-shape (Plate 583) introduced by Messrs Taylor & Kent Ltd. in 1972 was designed by Anthony Kusminck, Polish by birth with a French education. The firm's literature claims that the 'Kiln' shape 'bears no resemblance to any existing British design ... Tony Kusminek undertook the task of producing a range which would be unique in appearance but which would also indicate the influence of the Stoke-on-Trent surroundings ... and with admirable skill captured the original beauty and simplicity of these old ladies of industry (the old bottle-shaped kilns).... Production rationalisation and recent market research played an important role in standardising the lids for the tea and coffee pots and introducing a dual purpose cup for drinking both tea and coffee. The overall appearance of quality prevails, and the end product fulfils the original requirements of price and design efficiency, hence offering a fast running commodity of a design standard higher than usually provided by mass production techniques.' These publicity claims appear reasonable and this particular new design helps to show that mass-produced inexpensive ceramics can be attractive as well as functional.

In recent years there have been great changes in the Staffordshire Potteries; hardly one of the old kilns, remembered above, remains. The firing is carried out in long, tunnel kilns

424

through which the wares progress loaded on trolleys. The heat is generated by gas or electricity so that today the Staffordshire Potteries is a clean-air zone. The installation of modern machinery and the tunnel kilns is a costly business and the trend has been for firms to amalgamate and become part of large combines. Some of these amalgamations have embraced world-famous names—such as Minton's, now part of the Royal Doulton group. The Wedgwood Group includes Coalport and several pottery firms, such as William Adams.

While the individual names have been retained as has the individual character of the products, the formation of the large groups has enabled modern equipment to be installed, costs to be shared, and the new methods have materially helped to counteract the rising costs of raw materials and labour so that the modern wares are both functional and reasonably priced—two attributes which the commercial potter must always bear in mind.

It must not be thought that all modern pottery is the product of the Staffordshire Potteries. Many first-rate firms are situated in other places, and a section of these non-Staffordshire wares is shown in Plates 584–91. In general, these earthenwares and stonewares show more individuality than the Staffordshire wares and, of course, these country potteries are of smaller size than the leading Staffordshire firms. Some, in fact, could reasonably be called Studio Potteries.

The British commercial-pottery firms appear largely to neglect the purely decorative objects. No equivalent of the Victorian and earlier Staffordshire figure evidences itself, no national or international personalities are perpetuated in clay. However, some good animal models are produced. Babies and young children enjoy gaily designed mugs and plates having no parallel in earlier wares. There has been a tendency to produce special designs in limited issues—so ensuring a built-in rarity! Wedgwood's now make Christmas plates, and Spode Ltd. has a special department for commemorative wares. Some well-designed limited issues are the work of quite small firms or individuals. This type of product is here illustrated by two bowls from the Shand Kydd Pottery, a decorating and marketing concern rather than an actual manufacturing company.

It is too early to say if the new designs and shapes as featured in this last section will last, as have the oft-decried traditional wares. I am still undecided as to whether the commercial desire for change and novelty is a good or a bad thing, whether it has been responsible for poor designs or whether all progress can be attributed to this desire to market yet another new shape or motif.

Certainly I would perfer to eat from a simple modern plate, rather than a slip-decorated Toft-type dish, but each has its differing merits and are products of vastly different ages. We can surely admire the best of each.

583. Tasteful modern British tablewares, Kiln-shape, designed by Anthony Kusminck for Messrs Taylor & Kent, Ltd. of Longton. 1972.

584. Modern stoneware tea wares by Messrs Joseph Bourne & Son, Ltd. of Denby, reflecting perhaps the interest in Art Deco styles of the 1930s, see Plate 524. 1972.

585. Modern Denby oven-to-table stonewares of 'Romany' pattern designed by Glyn Colledge for Messrs Joseph Bourne & Son, Ltd. 1972.

586. A simple blue and white coffee-pot of 'Chatsworth' design made by Messrs Langley Pottery Ltd. 1972. 8¼ inches high.

587. A selection of oven-to-table stonewares made by Messrs T. G. Green & Co. Ltd. of Church Gresley, Derbyshire. 1972.

588. A simple and attractive 'Denby' oven-proof coffee pot of 'Greenwheat' pattern. 1972. $7\frac{1}{4}$ inches high.

589. A brown 'Denby' teapot of moulded 'Chevron' pattern produced by Messrs Joseph Bourne & Son, Ltd. 1972. $4\frac{1}{4}$ inches high.

590. A selection of simple table wares made by Messrs Henry Watson's Potteries, Ltd. of Wattisfield, Suffolk. 1972.

591. A selection of 'Suffolk Kitchen' ware by Messrs Henry Watson's Potteries, Ltd. of Wattisfield. Similar speckled glaze effect wares have been made over many years by several firms, see Plate 514. 1972.

592. Modern 'Nevada' range of wares in bright floral design as made by Hostess Tableware Ltd. of Longton, Staffordshire. 1972.

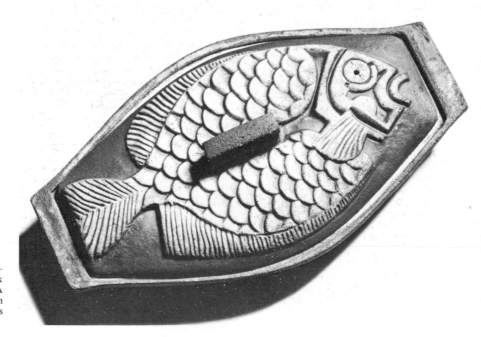

593. An unglazed stoneware oven-to-table fish-dish by 'Quantock Design' of Taunton, Somerset. A novel, decorative, range of such dishes are made. 1972. 14 inches long.

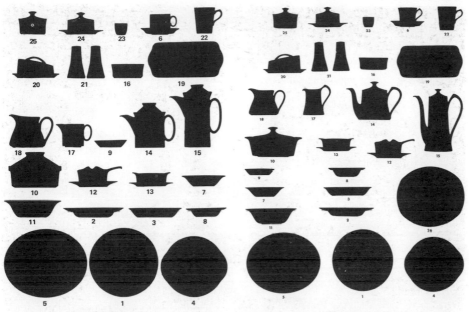

ANGLIA SHAPE
Modelled by Ernest Bailey

CONCORD SHAPE
Modelled by Ernest Bailey

594. A silhouette-chart of modern 'Anglia' (left) and 'Concord' (right) shapes produced in Staffordshire by Messrs Burgess & Leigh Ltd. of Burslem. 1972.

595. A covered tureen and stand of 'Castile' pattern on 'Anglia' shape, see above. 1972.

431

596. A selection of 'Stonehenge' range blue and white table wares by Messrs Midwinter Ltd. 1972.

597. A selection of the revived 'Lambeth-Stoneware' ovenproof table wares in 'Desert Night' design, by Messrs Royal Doulton Tablewares Ltd. 1972.

598. A selection of American-designed stoneware tablewares produced by 'Franciscan Tableware' of Hanley. 1972.

599. A selection of 'Mason's Ironstone' dinner wares, representing the traditional English designs and antique shapes. 1972.

600. A selection of Poole Pottery in the Aegean range designed by Leslie Elsden and produced in the Craft section of this commercial pottery. 1972.

601. A selection of Poole Pottery in the 'compact' range. The shapes are stackable and the ware oven-, detergent-, and dishwasher-proof! 1972.

434

602. A limited-issue Shakespeare subject punchbowl, one of several such designs issued under the name Shand Kydd Pottery and made in Staffordshire. 1971.

603. The interior of a numbered Shand Kydd Pottery special-issue punchbowl, showing the fine shape and superb printed design. 1971.

604. Two mugs and two money-boxes made by Messrs Josiah Wedgwood & Sons Ltd., to commemorate the investiture of the Prince of Wales at Caernarvon Castle in July 1969.

605. A special-issue Wedgwood Queen's Ware mug, the printed design commemorating the 900th anniversary of Lincoln Cathedral. A design commissioned by a local retailer—Francis Sinclair—and only available in Lincoln. 1972.

606. A Wedgwood special-issue Queen's Ware mug made to commemorate the Royal Silver Wedding. Designed by Professor Richard Guyatt, F.S.I.A. and available only in 1972.

607. The 'Bountiful Butterfly' calendar-plate in Wedgwood's Queen's Ware, one of a series started in 1971. This example was designed by a twenty-three-year-old student, Keith Manuel, at the Royal College of Art.

Guide to Dating

This is not a mark book, although several marks are reproduced at relevant points in the text. It is quite impossible to include here the whole range of marks, for at present there are well over four thousand British ceramic marks recorded, and specialist mark books such as my *Encyclopaedia of British Pottery and Porcelain Marks* (Herbert Jenkins, London, 1964) exceed seven hundred pages in length.

We can, however, conveniently list some of the general guidelines that should enable the non-expert to date a ceramic mark approximately—or at least to avoid the common error of ascribing a too early date. It is quite astounding how many people endeavour to date an object by adding together the ages of the various owners, conveniently overlooking the natural overlap of generations and assuming that the original owner acquired the object at birth!

The following guidelines will be found more reliable, but it should be remembered that they apply only to British pottery—not necessarily to porcelain.

> No impressed or printed name-mark will appear on pre-1755 wares.
>
> All printed marks denote a period after 1800.
>
> Any mark incorporating the name of the pattern, 'Willow', 'Rose', for example, will post-date 1810, and many are very much later.
>
> Marks incorporating the Royal Arms will be of post-1810 period.
>
> Examples bearing the diamond-shaped registration-mark (see page 442) are subsequent to 1842.
>
> Marks incorporating the word 'Limited' or the standard abbreviations 'Ltd' etc. indicate a date subsequent to the 1855 Act and in practice this coverage does not appear before the 1860s.
>
> The words 'Trade Mark' signify a date after 1862.
>
> The use of a prefix 'Royal' in the manufacturer's trade-name suggests a date after the middle of the nineteenth century.
>
> The occurrence of the abbreviation 'R^D No' (for registered number) followed by a series of numerals indicates a date after 1884 (see page 443).
>
> The occurrence of the word 'England' indicates a date after 1880, and generally after 1891, but not all late marks will include this word as it was required only on exported wares. It was required by foreign customs, not by our own officials.
>
> The wording 'Made in England' is purely a twentieth-century innovation, again only required on exported wares, so that its *absence* does *not* necessarily indicate an early date.
>
> Claims such as 'Detergent Proof' surely speak for themselves in evidencing a recent origin.

British Pottery

It should always be borne in mind that a date incorporated in a mark does not refer to the date of production. It normally relates to the year of establishment of that firm, or generally to a distantly related predecessor!

Much pottery of all periods was unmarked and the absence of a mark does not necessarily denote an early date. More often it simply means that the manufacturer had no reputation to trade upon, his name was not well known and the inclusion of a mark only slowed production and added marginally to the cost, without any likelihood of increasing the sale.

In closing these brief notes on marks and dating, I would refer my readers back to the *Introduction*, where my comments on these highly respected attributes are given.

PATENT OFFICE DESIGN REGISTRATION-MARKS

These marks are of diamond shape and appear (impressed, moulded or printed) on a variety of Victorian ware from 1842 to 1883. The purpose of this mark was to show that the design or shape had been registered with the Patent Office in London and was protected from copying by other manufacturers for an initial period of three years. It should be noted that this mark will therefore show the *earliest* date that an object bearing it could have been manufactured.

Two slightly different forms of arrangement were employed. The first, from 1842 to 1867, gives the year-letter in the top section. The second, from 1868 to 1883, has the year-letter at the right. The Roman numerals at the top denote the class of object: pottery and porcelain was Class IV.

This form of mark was discontinued in 1883. Subsequently, a simple progressive system of numbering was employed in which the registration-numbers were usually prefixed 'RᴰNo'. See page 443 for the key to this system.

REGISTRATION-MARKS

Below are the two patterns of Design Registration-Marks that were in current use between the years 1842 and 1883. Keys to 'year' and 'month' code-letters are given below.

The left-hand diamond was used during the years 1842 to 1867. A change was made in 1868, when the right-hand diamond was adopted.

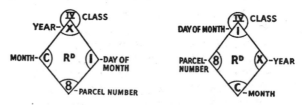

INDEX TO YEAR- AND MONTH-LETTERS

	YEARS 1842–67 *Year-Letter at Top*			1868–83 *Year-Letter at Top*	
A = 1845	N = 1864		A = 1871	L = 1882
B = 1858	O = 1862		C = 1870	P = 1877
C = 1844	P = 1851		D = 1878	S = 1875
D = 1852	Q = 1866		E = 1881	U = 1874

E = 1855	R = 1861	F = 1873	V = 1876
F = 1847	S = 1849	H = 1869	W = (Mar. 1–6)
G = 1863	T = 1867	I = 1872	1878
H = 1843	U = 1848	J = 1880	X = 1868
I = 1846	V = 1850	K = 1883	Y = 1879
J = 1854	W = 1865		
K = 1857	X = 1842		
L = 1856	Y = 1853		
M = 1859	Z = 1860		

MONTHS (BOTH PERIODS)

A = December

B = October

C or O = January

D = September

E = May

G = February

H = April

I = July

K = November (and December 1860)

M = June

R = August (and September 1–19 1857)

W = March

REGISTRATION-NUMBERS

Table of Design Registration-numbers found on wares first registered between January 1884 and 1909.

R^D No.   1 registered on 1 January 1884.

R^D No.   19754 registered on 1 January 1885.

R^D No.   40480 registered on 1 January 1886.

R^D No.   64520 registered on 1 January 1887.

R^D No.   90483 registered on 2 January 1888.

R^D No. 116648 registered on 1 January 1889.

R^D No. 141273 registered on 1 January 1890.

R^D No. 163767 registered on 1 January 1891.

R^D No. 185713 registered on 1 January 1892.

R^D No. 205240 registered on 2 January 1893.

R^D No. 224720 registered on 1 January 1894.

R^D No. 246975 registered on 1 January 1895.

R^D No. 268392 registered on 1 January 1896.

R^D No. 291241 registered on 1 January 1897.

R^D No. 311658 registered on 1 January 1898.

R^D No. 331707 registered on 2 January 1899.

R^D No. 351202 registered on 1 January 1900.

R^D No. 368154 registered on 1 January 1901.

R^D No. 385088 registered on 1 January 1902.

R^D No. 402913 registered on 1 January 1903.

R^D No. 425017 registered on 1 January 1904.

R^D No. 447548 registered on 2 January 1905.

R^D No. 471486 registered on 1 January 1906.

R^D No. 493487 registered on 1 January 1907.

R^D No. 518415 registered on 1 January 1908.

R^D No. 534963 registered on 1 January 1909.

Bibliography

This bibliography includes only those books which give a better than average coverage of the subject or include a large selection of helpful illustrations. It does not include the host of general books, most of which add little to our knowledge.

The specialist books are mentioned in the relevant sections, for example, books dealing with the Art Nouveau period are listed in that section, on page 347.

GENERAL BOOKS

BLACKER, J. F.
The A.B.C. of Nineteenth-Century Pottery & Porcelain. Stanley Paul & Co., London, n.d. *c.* 1911.

BLACKER, J. F.
The A.B.C. of English Salt-glaze Stoneware. Stanley Paul & Co., London, 1922.

BREARS, P. C. D.
The English Country Pottery, its History and Techniques. David & Charles, Newton Abbot, 1971.

BURTON, W.
A History & Description of English Earthenware & Stoneware. Cassell & Co., London, 1904.

GODDEN, G. A.
Illustrated Encyclopaedia of British Pottery and Porcelain. Herbert Jenkins, London, 1966.

HAGGAR, R. G.
English Country Pottery. Phoenix House Ltd., London, 1950.

HAGGAR, R. G. and MANKOWITZ, W.
The Concise Encyclopaedia of English Pottery and Porcelain. André Deutsch, London, 1957.

HONEY, W. B.
English Pottery and Porcelain. A. & C. Black, London, 5th edition, 1962.

HUGHES, G. B.
English & Scottish Earthenware. Lutterworth Press, London, 1961.

JEWITT, L.
The Ceramic Art of Great Britain. Virtue & Co., London, 1878 (revised 1883).

JEWITT, L.
The Ceramic Art of Great Britain, 1800–1900. Revised and re-illustrated by G. A. Godden, dealing only with the 1800–1900 period. Barrie & Jenkins, London, 1972.

LEWIS, G.
A Picture History of English Pottery. Hulton, London, 1956.

MILLER, J. JEFFERSON, II
English Yellow-Glazed Earthenware. Barrie & Jenkins, London, 1974 (announced).

RACKHAM, B. AND READ, H.
English Pottery. E. Benn Ltd., London, 1924. (Reprinted by E. P. Publishing Ltd., 1972.)

RHEAD, G. W. AND F. A.
Staffordshire Pots and Potters. Hutchinson & Co., London, 1906.

SANDON, H.
British Pottery and Porcelain for Pleasure and Investment. J. Gifford, London, 1969.

SHAW, S.
History of Staffordshire Potteries. Privately printed at Hanley, 1829.

TAGGART, ROSS E.
The Frank & Harriet Burnap Collection of English Pottery . . . Catalogue revised by Ross E. Taggart. Nelson Gallery, Atkins Museum, Kansas City, Missouri, 1967.

TOWNER, D.
English Cream-coloured Earthenware. Faber & Faber, London, 1957.

British Pottery

WAKEFIELD, H.
Victorian Pottery. Herbert Jenkins, London, 1962.

WARD, J.
History of the Borough of Stoke-upon-Trent. W. Lewis & Sons, London, 1843.

WEATHERILL, L.
The Pottery Trade and North Staffordshire, 1660–1760. Manchester University Press, 1971.

WILLIS, G.
English Pottery and Porcelain. Guinness Signatures, London, 1968.

BOOKS ON INDIVIDUAL FACTORIES OR WARES

Bristol
OWEN, H.
Two Centuries of Ceramic Art in Bristol. Bell & Daldry, London, 1873.

POUNTNEY, W. J.
The Old Bristol Potteries. J. Arrowsmith, Bristol, 1920. (Reprinted by E. P. Publishing Ltd., 1972.)

Delftware
CAIGER-SMITH, A.
Tin-Glaze Pottery in Europe and the Islamic World. Faber & Faber, London, 1973.

GARNER, F. H.
English Delftware. Faber & Faber, London, 1948, revised edition, 1972.

RAY, A.
English Delftware Pottery in the Robert Hall Warren Collection. Faber & Faber, London, 1968.
English Delftware Tiles. Faber & Faber, London, 1973.

Doulton
BLACKER, J. F.
The A.B.C. of English Salt-Glaze Stoneware. Stanley Paul, London, 1922.

EYLES, D.
Royal Doulton, 1815–1965. Hutchinson, London, 1965.

Leeds
TOWNER, D.
English Cream-coloured Earthenware. Faber & Faber, London, 1957.

TOWNER, D.
The Leeds Pottery. Cory, Adams & Mackay, London, 1963.

Liverpool
SMITH, A.
The Illustrated Guide to Liverpool Herculaneum Pottery. Barrie & Jenkins, London, 1970.

Marks
CHAFFERS, W.
Marks & Monograms ... 15th edition, revised by G. A. Godden, Vol. II, British Section. William Reeves, London, 1965.

GODDEN, G. A.
Encyclopaedia of British Pottery and Porcelain Marks. Herbert Jenkins, London, 1964.

RHEAD, G. W.
British Pottery Marks. Scott, Greenwood & Son, London, 1910.

Mason's
GODDEN, G. A.
The Illustrated Guide to Mason's Ironstone China. Barrie & Jenkins, London, 1971.

HAGGAR, R. G.
The Masons of Lane Delph. Percy Lund Humphries & Co. Ltd., 1951.

Printed wares in Underglaze Blue
COYSH, A. W.
Blue and White Transfer Ware, 1780–1840. David & Charles, Newton Abbot, 1970.

LITTLE, W. L.
Staffordshire Blue. Batsford, London, 1969.

WILLIAMS, S. B.
Antique Blue and White Spode. Batsford, London, 1943.

Rockingham
EAGLESTON, A. AND LOCKETT, T. A.
The Rockingham Pottery. Rotherham Library & Museum, 1964.

Scottish Pottery
FLEMING, J. A.
Scottish Pottery. Maclehose, Jackson & Co., Glasgow, 1923.

Spode
WHITER, L.
Spode, A History of the Family Factory and Wares from 1733–1833. Barrie & Jenkins, London, 1970.

WILLIAMS, S. B.
Antique Blue and White Spode. Batsford, London, 1943.

Staffordshire figures
BALSTON, T.
Staffordshire Portrait Figures of the Victorian Age. Faber & Faber, London, 1958.

HAGGAR, R. G.
Staffordshire Chimney Ornaments. Phoenix House Ltd., London, 1955.

HALL, J.
Staffordshire Portrait Figures. Charles Letts & Co. Ltd., London, 1972.

OLIVER, A.
The Victorian Staffordshire Figure: a Guide for Collectors. Heinemann, London, 1971.

PUGH, P. D. G.
Staffordshire Portrait Figures. Barrie & Jenkins, London, 1971.

STANLEY, L. T.
Collecting Staffordshire Pottery. W. H. Allen, London, 1963.

Studio Pottery

BIRKS, T.
The Art of the Modern Pottery. Country Life, London, 1967.

COOPER, R. G.
The Modern Potter. Tiranti Ltd., London, 1947.

DIGBY, G. W.
The Work of the Modern Potter in England. Murray, London, 1952.

ROSE, M.
Artist Potters in England. Faber & Faber, London, 1955. Revised edition, 1970.

Swansea

NANCE, E. M.
The Pottery and Porcelain of Swansea and Nantgarw. Batsford, London, 1942.

Wedgwood

HONEY, W. B.
Wedgwood Ware. Faber & Faber, London, 1948.

KELLY, A.
Wedgwood Ware. Ward Lock, London, 1970.

MANKOWITZ, W.
Wedgwood. Dutton & Co., New York, 1953.

Many other specialist books on Wedgwood give a good account of this firm and its wares and illustrate various examples, see page 114.

In addition, serious collectors will no doubt find interesting learned papers included in the *Transactions of the English Ceramic Circle* (published for the E.C.C. by Messrs Cory Adams & Mackay Ltd., Fair Row, Chatham, Kent) and interesting articles on ceramics will be found from time to time in the various collectors' magazines most of which are published monthly. These include:

Antiques, an American monthly published in New York.
Antiques Collector, a British monthly.
Collector's Guide, a British monthly.
The Connoisseur, a British monthly.

Other magazines such as *The Burlington Magazine* and *Country Life* can also contain articles of interest on ceramics.

Index

7. 1. JL